The Baby Boomer's Guide

TO A

Rockin' & Rollin' Retirement

DRIFT AWAY

"Oh give me the beat boys to free my soul
I wanna get lost in your rock & roll
And drift away."
Dobie Gray (1973)

"Oh give me the beat boys to free my soul
I wanna get lost in your rock & roll
And drift away....into retirement."
Baby Boomers (2016)

The Baby Boomer's Guide to a Rockin' & Rollin' Retirement

"What a great resource for retirement planning! This guide gives a fun yet informative look into strategies for retirement that most people don't think of taking advantage of. I loved being taken back in time with many of the great rock hits brought up in each chapter."

—*Dan Allison, president and founder of Feedback Marketing Group*

"Danny's book is a breath of fresh air for baby boomers planning for their retirement. As a fellow baby boomer who by day helps advisors work with their clients, and by night has been a rock musician for thirty-plus years, I really appreciate and can relate to Danny's creative way of blending rockin' roll with retirement."

—*Kim Dorr, special accounts manager at Brokers Clearing House LTD*

"I wish I had this information years ago. Your financial knowledge with the reference to classic rock made for an incredible read, which I found very helpful."

—*Bob Earley, concert promoter / radio host*

"What a great read! This book contains 'must-have' information for all of us baby boomers about retirement planning.

The book combines retirement tools with awesome classic rock song titles, song lyrics, and commonsense analogies. Danny speaks from the heart on his real-life experiences and valuable lessons we can all learn from. This book has a very unique twist on a very hot topic: retirement.

Brilliant!"

—Jay Van Beusekom, RHU, LUTCF, president & CEO
of Jay Van Beusekom Financial Advisor, LLC

"As a certified baby boomer three years away from retirement and someone who loves the music of the boomer generation, I find this book to be a practical blueprint for retirement planning. As the Moody Blues sang of 'The Days of Future Past,' I think of how quickly forty years of working life has passed. Whether I am singing 'Here Comes the Sun' on a warm Arizona winter day or 'I'm a Believer,' my life has been enriched because I started planning for retirement forty years ago with a pay-myself-first philosophy. And now I look at my plans and sing, 'I'll pay you back with interest.'

I encourage you to read this book and act on the recommendations. Of course, I would have music playing in the background. How about 'It's Now or Never'?"

—Herb Hames, development director
Father Flanagan's Boys Home, Boys Town, Nebraska

"Danny's book speaks to all of us baby boomers thinking about retirement, in the language of the music we grew up with. He lays out very readable guidelines for having a successful retirement and punctuates them with sad, funny, and relevant stories we can all relate to. Who knew that the rock lyrics of our youth pointed the way to a good retirement? I guess Danny did, and with his book we all can too!"

—*Stephen E. Alloy, J.D. MBA CLU ChFC MSFS*
Advanced Markets Specialist

"This is really a fun and entertaining, easy read that causes you to think throughout with an occasional 'ahha', that really makes sense! Danny's rock and roll theme really speaks to the boomer generation in particular but is something that younger generations may connect with as well.

His point that products are not plans really struck a chord with me, as I couldn't agree more deeply with him on that point. You need a plan. Your favorite NFL team's coaches don't look at each other on Sunday afternoon after the national anthem and say, 'So what do you think we should do today?' No, they've been game planning all week, and you should start your game planning ideally about ten years prior to your retirement.

Follow Danny's thoughts and ideas and use them to question your own beliefs. I'll end with this thought, 'It's not what you don't know that can hurt you, it's what you know to be absolutely true that isn't, which can hurt you.'"

—*Martin V. Higgins, CFP, CLU, AEP*

"I'm happy Danny Smith has compiled this work filled with financial expertise and rock 'n roll memories and trivia. Having co-hosted a radio show with Danny, I know and appreciate his knowledge and passion for both the financial/investing industry and the oldies but goodies. I'm very pleased to be a small part of his work."

—*Wally Mintus, WDLW Radio, "Kool Kat" 1380, Oberlin*

"When I met Danny a few years ago at an event in Munich, Germany, we immediately 'bonded' (no pun intended). That's because we share a love for basketball, good music, and helping others on the road to success—while trying to have fun doing it! As a professional speaker I always mention the vital role that my coach, Clem Haskins, has played in helping me to be my best as a college and NBA player and as a professional speaker. Danny's book can help coach you to a rockin' and rollin' and hopefully happy retirement!"

—*Walter Bond, speaker, author, former NBA player*
www.walterbond.com

"Combining the wisdom found in songs which define the boomers 'soundtrack of our lives' with the message of financial responsibility, Danny has created an insightful and enjoyable book that will have readers 'dog-earing' pages and learning valuable lessons. Find a comfortable chair, load up some tunes, and discover that it really is possible to create the life you truly want."

— *Robert Gignac, author,* Rich is a State of Mind

Dedication

*To my mom "Winnie" Smith who somehow kept a roof over our heads
when "the big bad wolf" showed up at our door in 1955*

To my wife Brenda for her love and support

*To my two wonderful daughters Jennifer and Jessica and their kids
Jazmine and Julian who have brought such joy to our lives*

To my late brother, Tim, who we lost way too soon

*To Baby Boomers worldwide who grew up during the era of "classic rock"
and have kept on rockin' ever since!*

The Baby Boomer's Guide

TO A

Rockin' & Rollin' Retirement

DANNY SMITH

Published by Advantage, Charleston, South Carolina.
Member of Advantage Media Group.

ADVANTAGE is a registered trademark and the Advantage colophon is a trademark of Advantage Media Group, Inc.

Printed in the United States of America.

ISBN: 978-1-59932-700-6
LCCN: 2016941245

Book design by Matthew Morse.

This publication is designed to provide accurate and authoritative information in regard to the subject matter covered. It is sold with the understanding that the publisher is not engaged in rendering legal, accounting, or other professional services. If legal advice or other expert assistance is required, the services of a competent professional person should be sought.

Advantage Media Group is proud to be a part of the Tree Neutral® program. Tree Neutral offsets the number of trees consumed in the production and printing of this book by taking proactive steps such as planting trees in direct proportion to the number of trees used to print books. To learn more about Tree Neutral, please visit **www.treeneutral.com.** To learn more about Advantage's commitment to being a responsible steward of the environment, please visit **www.advantagefamily.com/green**

Advantage Media Group is a publisher of business, self-improvement, and professional development books and online learning. We help entrepreneurs, business leaders, and professionals share their Stories, Passion, and Knowledge to help others Learn & Grow. Do you have a manuscript or book idea that you would like us to consider for publishing? Please visit **advantagefamily.com** or call **1.866.775.1696.**

Contents

Talkin' 'Bout My Generation

People try to put us down, just because we get around.
—*"My Generation," The Who (1965)*

When Pete Townshend wrote the lyrics to "My Generation," he had no idea how influential it would be. The song crossed international borders and united an entire generation, and the passion of that song still inspires listeners today. Lead singer Roger Daltrey still sings the famous line, "I hope I die before I get old," with as much heart as he did in his early twenties, even if it is a little tongue-in-cheek now that he's in his seventies.

Most baby boomers believe as I do that although aging is inevitable, "getting old" isn't. We're living life in a way that our parents and grandparents never imagined. My generation, the baby boomers, are moving into the greatest era of our lives, and we're coming at it not as our parents did, with little expectation beyond a pension, a rocking chair, and maybe a garden or a bingo club; we are doing it differently. We're following our dreams and redefining the status quo of retirement as much as we redefined the music world with rock 'n' roll.

What Does Retirement Really Mean To You?

There's a great tune on the early Rolling Stones album *December's Children* called "I'm Free." I think the words speak to the way many baby boomers view their personal retirement: "I'm free to do what I want any old time. So love me, hold me, love me, hold me. I'm free any old time to get what I want."

If you're ready to retire but not ready to stop rockin' and rollin', then it's time to start plannin'! As a financial advisor, my job is to find out *what retirement means* for my clients. If you have not taken the time to think about this, now is the time. There is no such thing as a cookie-cutter retirement anymore. As your advisor, I can help you design your own *personal retirement plan* so that, to paraphrase Mick and Keith, you may be free any old time to do what you want in retirement. Because once you've envisioned your ideal retirement, you're going to need to plan financially to make it happen.

Not long ago, I met a man with a rather unique perspective on retirement. It was on my way back from a convention hosted by a major insurance company and, as a guest speaker, they'd hired a limo to take me back to the airport. On the way there, the fellow driving the limo made me feel like the most important passenger he'd ever had in his car—and after a while, I asked him how long he'd been driving limos for a living.

"Two weeks," he said. "I just retired about two months ago."

I was shocked. "Where did you retire from?" I asked.

It turned out he had worked as an executive for a well-known Fortune 500 company and was following in the footsteps of a friend and fellow executive retiree of the same company. That friend had become bored soon after retiring and wanted to do something with his time, so he reached out to the man who owned this limo company.

"He started to drive a limo and told me it was the most fun he'd had in the last twenty years," the driver said. "So when I got bored a few weeks after I retired, I asked him if I could join him. Now I'm driving a limo."

"Can you make any money driving a limo?" I asked.

"I don't even know how much money I'm making at this," he said and laughed. "We haven't figured that out yet. I just wanted to stay busy in retirement."

I was surprised. Even though he was working, the limo driver's new "job" was his ideal retirement. He got to meet new people and work in a relatively low-stress environment, and it kept him from getting bored. He was experiencing more joy "working" for the limo company than he did as an executive.

Limo driving, of course, is not everyone's ideal way of spending his or her retirement. Some retirees may prefer a life of travel and adventure, relaxation and luxury, getting their kicks road tripping down Route 66 in an RV or finding a vibrant community where they can live a life of leisure.

Are You Planning for Life?

The future's uncertain and the end is always near.
—*"Roadhouse Blues," The Doors (1970)*

While Jim Morrison's prophetic words were accurate in describing his personal outlook and all-too-short life, the fact is that baby boomers are living far longer than earlier generations, which means that instead of planning for years of retirement, we're planning for *decades*. And with each of us having a unique definition of retirement, like my limo-driving friend, and a unique desire of how we want to live out retirement, an advisor can help us stay on our unique course through retirement, or—as Morrison would say—someone who can help "keep your eyes on the road and your hands upon the wheel."

Your retirement future should be certain enough that you can comfortably "let it roll baby roll . . . let it roll all night long." Unless, of course, you're like me and go to bed before ten o'clock!

Undoubtedly, you have worked hard for many years, whether with a company or running your own business. During that time, you have likely done some type of retirement investing, whether it's through a 401(k), an IRA, or personal investments. If you have, I congratulate you!

But the fact is that your 401(k), IRA, personal investments, and insurance policies are *products*, not plans. Many people may think they have a plan, but what they really have is a group of products purchased incrementally and at different times that have not been coordinated to work together to achieve the highest probability of success. Have you ever looked at something that you purchased impulsively and thought, *What could I have been thinking?* I have—usually with clothing that ended up hanging unworn in the closet. Similarly, every financial product should have a defined purpose within your plan because *products without purpose* can be counterproductive.

Think of it as a puzzle, and as the Average White Band put it, we need to "pick up the pieces" and put them together. The key, however, is the picture on the puzzle box, which you need so you know where the pieces go and what the puzzle will look like when it is finished. Like Ringo Starr lamented in his 1973 hit "Photograph," "Every time I see your face, it reminds me of the places we used to go. But all I got is a photograph."

Your retirement is that photograph, and instead of thinking of it as a faded memory or impossible dream, you need to believe in it and make it happen. The investments you have made and the products you have purchased are the puzzle pieces. What I can do is help you figure out where all the pieces go as we work toward the picture on the box. But first, you need to know what the picture looks like.

When I decided to write this book, my goal was to make it a fun-to-read quick-start guide that helps to point you in the right direction and, unlike Jim Morrison, have a retirement future with as little uncertainty as possible. Well, maybe I can help. I've been assisting people with identifying and managing their risks and long-term financial objectives for more than thirty-five years. But perhaps more importantly, I am one of you. I am a fellow baby boomer who grew up listening to the same music as many of my clients, watching the same television shows, experiencing the same historical, turbulent, and exciting events of the sixties.

The passion I have for this business is centered on my desire to help my clients be as prepared as possible for all that life has to offer them before and after retirement, and a big part of that is showing them, not telling them. I take my work very seriously, but I like to have fun doing it. When you come to my office, you will not find CNBC on the television and the latest Dow Jones Averages scrolling below. What does that "noise" have to do with a potential twenty- or thirty-year retirement? Instead, we do everything we can to keep our office comfortable and laid back, even going so far as to include a "Discovery Session" before you decide to work with us. During this session, no business is transacted other than getting to know each other. I guess you could call it a "continuity test" in that I simply want to make sure that if we do team up on your retirement plan, you understand what you can expect from us and us from you. Most importantly, however, I want to make sure that we get along. Remember the Turtle's hit "Happy Together"? Well, at this point in my career, I limit my practice to working with "happy people" who are looking for a long-term partnership with their advisor. That's why even after thirty-five years I can say that I look forward to coming to work every day. I speak from the heart when I say, "I love what I do!"

Why I Made Financial Planning My Lifelong Passion . . . Apart from Classic Rock and Roll

Little pigs, little pigs, let me in, or I'll huff and I'll puff and I'll blow your house in.

Remember the classic 1933 Disney cartoon "The Three Little Pigs"? Our little grandson Julian loves to watch it with me, and it's easy to find on YouTube. The story is one I often relate to when speaking with groups throughout the country. It's the story of a house that in the blink of an eye turned into a house of straw when the Big Bad Wolf knocked.

Back in 1955 I had no way of knowing that the Smith family home in Lorain, Ohio, was going to experience a similar real-life story. Our financial house seemed solid enough to me (as a five-year-old), my mom, and my two brothers. That is, until the figurative Big Bad Wolf knocked on our door and blew the house down. I can still recall my mom rushing upstairs to dad's side when she heard him gasping for air, and although she was a registered nurse, it was too late. He died of a massive heart attack. I have only a few fond memories of my father because he died so young, but there is a glaringly sad one; he left us virtually destitute.

My dad had no life insurance, and my mother was left with three boys to raise on her own with no nest egg. I don't know how she managed to keep a roof over our heads, but she did. What I know now, but I didn't know then, was the devastating toll that my father's death took on Mom. The challenges she faced led her to what I now know to be depression. That depression led to alcohol abuse, and by her early seventies, she was worn out. She died at what I consider to be a young age.

Thinking back to those days inspires me as I work with each of my clients, regardless of their ages, to help ensure that they are financially prepared for what life has in store for them—good and bad. If you only remember me for one thing, I hope it's this: When a parent dies young, like my dad did, life insurance is often the difference between a financially secure family and one that struggles financially.

I also want my clients to be able to enjoy life after retirement. They may have various assets, or what I call "buckets" of money, earmarked for retirement. They think, *Hey, I'm going to use this to go places and buy things.*

However, if you do not take the time to properly plan it all out with a trusted advisor, one or all of those buckets of money could end up empty because of what I call the *Risk of the Great Unknown*, a topic which I go into more in chapter 3 but which is basically the future health-care expenses brought on by illness, injury, or old-age frailty.

Instead of keeping those buckets separate, consider what we could do if we brought them together, took a look at how they're working, and determined if there might be methods to increase their long-term potential while at the same time reduce immediate and long-term risks.

The important thing to remember is that with planning, it's never too soon to begin, and it's never too late to start over again. So when people ask me what the first step is in the planning process, I reply, "Let's sit down and try to figure out what you're trying to do!"

The next part of that process is when I ask certain rhetorical questions that I hope will make people pause and ponder. For example, let's imagine that I'm sitting down for the first time with a couple, John and Mary. I ask, "Mary, have you thought about what your world will look like financially if John died suddenly early into retirement?" Or, "If one of you requires custodial care in the future, do you have a plan in place to pay for it?" Even after thirty-five-plus years, I have never had anyone respond, "Oh yes, Danny, we have thought that out and have it completely under control."

When thinking about retirement, consider that for most of us there are three stages that everyone needs to prepare for:

1. The go-go years
2. The slow-go years
3. The no-go years

A good financial advisor will help you plan to maximize your retirement-years opportunities on the front end, during the go-go years, help you do as much as you're able to do in the mid-term or slow-go years, and help ensure that you've reserved enough for your care and well-being during the no-go years.

Even if you feel as though you have sufficient assets for your future, this does not mean you're completely prepared for all three of those retirement stages. If you do not have the proper safeguards in place, you can lose the money you worked so long and so hard for very quickly. Take it from me, it only takes one visit from the Big Bad Wolf for "the walls to come tumblin' down," as John Mellencamp would put it.

Superstar David Crosby is a prime example of a Big Bad Wolf victim. One of the most successful musicians in our generation, who rose to fame in the midsixties with bands such as the Byrds and Crosby, Stills, and Nash (and sometimes Young), was broke by the 1980s. In that brief time, he'd made and spent about $25 million. His situation may be at the extreme end of poor financial planning, but it goes to show how poor decisions and planning can result in losing, literally, millions of dollars.

Rock and roll's "first great wild man" Jerry Lee Lewis is another example of a successful musician who went from earning $10,000 a concert at the peak of his career to owing the IRS more than $3 million in back taxes by the 1980s.

There are countless additional examples of musicians, actors, and sports stars who rose to fame quickly, acquired more money than most of us could ever dream of, and then quickly lost it due to poor planning, bad choices, and associating with untrustworthy advisors. It can happen to anyone. I will discuss this more and give you additional examples of risk in chapter 3.

Creating the Path to a Successful Retirement

You who are on the road must have a code that you
can live by, and so become yourself . . .
—*"Teach Your Children," Crosby, Stills, Nash & Young (1970)*

This book starts off with an important subject, something that we think about more and more as we grow older and as we think about our past and our future: time. Some might say that time is the most valuable currency there is—you only get so much of it, and once you use it, it is gone. In chapter 2, we will talk about money. This might seem like a simple subject— we all know what money *does*, but how much do you really know about what it *is*? After that, in chapter 3, I'll share with you the types of risks we face as we grow older and plan for retirement. In chapters 4 and 5, I delve into the value of life insurance and other types of insurance you should consider based on factors like personal risks.

In chapter 6, we will look at investments and my philosophy on investing, as well as some tips and strategies. After that, I will discuss life's choices, changes, challenges, and detours, followed by a chapter addressing the life events that many of us go through: buying a house, marriage, kids, divorce, and career. Chapter 8 delves into the importance of leaving a legacy and philanthropy, and chapter 9 tackles the inevitability of taxes and alternative ways to look at them. Finally, we'll close with the importance of asset planning for long-term care events. If you plan on living a long life, you do not want to skip this chapter.

Throughout this book, I hope to bring back some good memories for you, with references to the classic rock and roll we grew up with in the 1960s and 1970s. At the end of each chapter, you will see a suggested-listening playlist. While it is essential that we think about our futures, it is also beneficial and fun to think about what shaped who we are today. The music of the sixties and seventies was about expression, rebellion, and independence and opened our eyes to the once-taboo subjects of war, drugs, sex, culture, peace, government, death, and politics. I hope that by including references to my favorite musicians and tunes, I can motivate you to think about and discuss the taboo subjects in this book—death, illness, aging—and embrace the inevitable. Because as long as you have a plan and an idea of what you want for the future, these subjects become much easier to handle and to approach with a sense of empowerment. With confidence, education, and a trusted advisor, you may have the rockin' and rollin' retirement you deserve.

Playlist:

1. "Rockin' Down the Highway," The Doobie Brothers (1972)
2. "Takin' Care of Business," Bachman-Turner Overdrive (1973)
3. "Take It Easy," The Eagles (1972)
4. "The Best Is Yet to Come," Frank Sinatra (1958)
5. "(Get Your Kicks on) Route 66," Multiple artists
6. "We May Never Pass This Way Again," Seals & Croft (1973)
7. "Leaving on a Jet Plane," Peter, Paul, and Mary (1969)
8. "Dock of the Bay," Otis Redding (1967)
9. "Come on Let's Go," Richie Valens (1959)
10. "We've Only Just Begun" The Carpenters (1970)
11. "My Generation" The Who (1965)
12. "Teach Your Children," Crosby, Stills, Nash & Young (1970)
13. "Roadhouse Blues," The Doors (1970)

CHAPTER 1:

Time is on My Side . . . or Is It?

You're searching for good times, but just wait and see.
You'll come runnin' back to me . . . Time is on my side, yes, it is.
—*"Time is On My Side," The Rolling Stones (1964)*

If you're "searching for good times" in retirement, the best advice I can give is *please start planning now!* I believe that the key component to successful retirement is taking the time to plan for it and—to paraphrase the Rolling Stones early hit—time *is* on your side unless you wait too long. Procrastination is the nemesis of successful outcomes because either you never get started or you get started too late. There are consequences for this. For every preretirement year you let slip by without investing in your future, you could set yourself back three to five successful postretirement years down the road. Planning a sound personal retirement strategy is not something to do tomorrow. You need to do it now, today, before more time slips away.

Doctor, Doctor Give Me the News

If you were told, like I was a few years ago, that a cyst on your neck, which was originally diagnosed as benign, had spread to your lymph nodes and developed into stage-four cancer, would you just wait to see what happens next, or would you do what I did and immediately ask, "What do we need to do about it now?"

You would get started as soon as possible, of course. Waiting will not make it better, and planning for retirement should be approached with the same sense of urgency. There is no extra time to mull it over.

At the same time, it's often wise not to take a do-it-yourself approach to financial planning.

My friend, Robert Gignac, who is a best-selling author and sought-after speaker based in Toronto, Canada, is not in the financial-services business, but he encourages people to avoid the do-it-yourself approach to financial planning with this example from his book *Rich is a State of Mind*:

"In Toronto, Canada, there is a medical-supply company that rents virtually every type of medical equipment that you can think of. Anyone can walk in, and without any proof of medical experience or accreditation, rent anything—including all of the devices needed to perform a do-it-yourself root canal! All you need then is the instruction manual and you're good to go."

Who would do that?

Having all the right equipment and instructions doesn't mean you can do your own root canal or surgery. In January of 2012 I went for outpatient surgery to have a "benign" cyst removed from my neck. When I awoke in the recovery room my surgeon was standing next to me. I recall thinking, *Why is she here?* When she spoke, her words hit me like a ton of bricks. "Danny, we found something we weren't looking for—a lymph node loaded with cancer. We need to begin immediate treatment!" She explained that sometimes a biopsy can miss its mark. And that's what happened with me. I went in to have a forty-five-minute walk-away procedure and woke up 2.5 hours later to be told that I was in stage 4 cancer. Wow! When the shock wore off I sought out a reputable oncologist. I certainly didn't try to treat myself, and most people will agree with that—if you're in need of professional medical treatment, you immediately seek out properly trained physicians and medical facilities.

When it comes to finances and planning, I have no objection to people trying to learn everything they can about it. In fact, I encourage you to do so. I made it a point to learn everything I could about the type of cancer I had, including the effects of heavy-duty radiation on my neck. But I let my doctors and the professionals at the treatment center do the heavy lifting.

For something as important as your financial future—which in reality is the rest of your life—I encourage you to do the same!

The Biggest Graveyard in the World is the Graveyard of Lost Opportunity

If you haven't started planning, however, there's no need to panic. It is never too late to sit down with an advisor and start looking at where you are and how you can take advantage of the time you do have. "The time has come today," Willie and Joe Chambers wrote in their 1968 acid rock anthem of the same name. These guys were probably not thinking about retirement when they wrote these lyrics, but they certainly ring true in this book.

I have seen it countless times—people retire and think they will be fine. And for the first year, five years, maybe even ten years, they'll probably be okay. Nobody runs out of money in their first year after retirement. The danger is in failing to recognize the potential longevity of retirement. After ten years, you might still have a lot of tread left on your tires, but what if you run out of money? You end up with an empty gas tank and not enough money to support your lifestyle.

This is why time is of the essence to any plan. As much as the popular phrase "saving time" might suggest, you can't save time the way you save money. You can spend fifty cents of a dollar and "save" the other fifty cents, but you can't spend twelve hours in a day and save the other twelve for a rainy day. So with this chapter, I want to help change your mind-set and teach you how to spend your time wisely by planning ahead.

When I Learned about the Value of Time and Money

Old man, look at my life, I'm a lot like you were. Old man,
look at my life, twenty-four and there's so much more.
—*"Old Man," Neil Young (1972)*

When I was twenty-four years old, I met a man who did me one of the greatest favors of my life, and that was to teach me the value of time and money.

I was working as an assistant manager at a retail store just outside of Elmira, New York, when the manager pointed out that this fellow was passing his business card out in the store, which we did not allow.

"Go give that guy the boot," the manager told me, and I went down to the sales floor to politely ask him to leave.

He was nice, and on his way out, he said, "You look like a bright young man. I'm with an investment company called IDS. Letter I, letter D, letter S. I'll leave, but let me give you my card. If you're ever in Elmira, I'll buy you lunch."

For whatever reason, I took him up on his offer of lunch—maybe because no one had ever offered to buy me lunch before. During that lunch he explained to me how a mutual fund worked, and I agreed to start my own, investing what he described as a dollar a day, or thirty dollars a month.

The next day I called him and said, "I gave it a little thought. I can do a dollar and a quarter a day. Let's do forty dollars a month."

I also promised him that I would commit to saving this amount every month for the next fifteen years. No matter where I moved, that amount was taken out of my checking. For many of those years, the market was flat or went down, but toward the end, it started to consistently go up.

My account grew to more than $30,000. To this day I have that first confirmation of forty dollars being invested into the fund from my checking account.

I also still have that man's business card all these years later: E.R. Joseph. I'm not sure if he's still living, but if he walked into my office today, I'd hug him and thank him for giving me the best education I could have had as a young man. If it hadn't been for him coming into the store when he did and I hadn't been the one to tell him to leave, I would never have met him, and I never would have started on my personal retirement strategy until far later in life.

He taught me that it's not about the amount but the amount of time. Thanks, Mr. Joseph, wherever you are!

Put Me in, Coach!

Put me in, coach, I'm ready to play today.
—*"Centerfield," John Fogerty (1985)*

The value of having a coach, whether it's in life, finances, or playing the game, cannot be understated.

I've been playing pickup basketball for most of my adult life, which I enjoy for the exercise. I meet many new people, and from time to time have a few cold ones with the guys afterward. In pickup games, captains choose from a pool of players—usually anybody who shows up and wants to play. There are no set rosters. I've never played on a "team" in the true sense, though I've earned the basketball nickname "Smitty" from the many friends I have made over the years playing on the hardwood.

A few years back we made it a point to regularly go to Cleveland to scrimmage an adult-league team that our friends played on. Even though our pickup team, man-for-man, had superior size, speed, and skill, their team won more often than not because they had two things that we didn't have: a coach and a game plan. While we were just playing they were *running plays.* Their coach watched us like a hawk, judged our strengths and weaknesses, and used that to devise a winning game-plan strategy.

As an advisor, I also try to coach my clients to successful long-term outcomes. I don't come after them with a whistle and make them run laps, but I do try to coach them to the best of my abilities and work with them to create a game plan that has a better chance of success.

What I don't do, however, is tell them what their goals should be. Rather, I want to know what goals they have. Do they like to travel? What about family? How do they feel about their retirement-planning process so far? How do they think I might be able to help them improve their probability of having a successful retirement?

It's not just about how much money you think you'll need in retirement but how much income you'll need to match your financial obligations. In helping our clients plan for retirement, we address whether or not they have an income base that equals their expected expenses throughout their retirement, adjusted for inflation. If the worst thing happens and all their investments go down the tubes, they still have that income flow that was put into protected instruments such as annuities.

My role is not to take over their retirement but to serve as the captain of their personal retirement ship, helping to guide them through the ocean of retirement. There will be many days of smooth sailing, but there will also be the inevitable storms or even a hurricane. It's when the rough waters start kicking up that I can really fulfill my obligation as a good captain, guiding my clients' ships through the storm with the least amount of discomfort possible.

One example of this happened several years ago when a couple came into my office and said, "Danny, we want to take our whole family to Hawaii, but we're not sure we can afford it."

I had been telling them for the longest time that they should do something like that. They had the assets, but if they kept putting it off, I was concerned that they might eventually run out of time. So I helped them plan their trip. I even introduced them to a good friend and travel agent who set it all up for them.

Before they left, however, I made them promise me that on the first night after arriving in Hawaii, they would spend that night together as a family. "With all this loveliness, there should be love," as Elvis Presley put it so well in his 1961 song, "Blue Hawaii."

I suggested they do this because once they arrived, everyone was going to want to do different things, and there probably wouldn't be another chance for everyone to get together. I also suggested that they designate someone to take pictures to commemorate the event, as this was back before the advent of smartphones and their handy cameras.

I arranged a conference room for them to meet in at the hotel where they were staying, and I suggested they ask every family member to bring with them a happy memory of grandma and granddad.

"Tell them that is the only thing that's asked of them in exchange for your generosity," I said.

Months later, my secretary let me know that the couple was coming into the office. I met them in the lobby, and the wife immediately came up and hugged me. In her hand, she held a photo album. She flipped to a picture of her whole family in Hawaii.

"That first night, we did what you suggested, and it is the most memorable night we have ever had as a family," she said with tears on her face. "It's the best thing we ever did. I don't know how to thank you for the memories you helped us create."

This "magic night of nights" is just one example of what can happen when you take the time to make a plan. This couple was able to come to me as their advisor, and I was able to assure them they had the funds to take this trip and create wonderful family memories without worrying about money. This is the value of planning—of taking all the assets, investments, and products you have for retirement and fitting them into a plan.

As an advisor, I guide and encourage my clients to use some of their money to first focus on creating *wealthy memories* during their lifetime rather than *wealthy beneficiaries* after they're gone. Even though I probably lived by the Grass Roots' tune "Live for Today" a little more than I should have back in the midsixties, the advice to "live for today and don't worry about tomorrow" is probably *not* something I would pass on to my kids and grandkids . . . though I had one hell of a time trying it out back then!

Keep The Good Times Rolling

Remember that catchy late 1950s tune by Shirley and Lee, "Let the Good Times Roll"? It's one of those tunes that, once you hear it, it stays with you for a while—sometimes even jostling you out of a good sleep at three o'clock in the morning. In retirement, there's one thing I can say for certain: the good times stop rolling when the money runs out. My job is to help make sure that doesn't happen to you.

So what can you do to make the most of your time? First and foremost, realize that a team does better with a coach and a game plan. Whether or not you consider yourself to be a financially savvy person, you likely will benefit from sitting down with an expert, explaining your view of retirement, and seeing how far along the line you are to accomplishing a successful retirement. Think back on some of the most successful classic rock bands and musicians from our generation—the Rolling Stones' first manager, Andrew Loog Oldham, was just nineteen years old when he hooked up with the Stones. He was the one who saw the Stones' potential as the "anti-Beatles" band, even though John and Paul actually wrote the group's second single "I Wanna be Your Man." Or what about The Beatles' long-time producer George Martin? Without him, who knows how far the Beatles would have gone? The Stones, the Beatles, and countless others acquired much of their success because they were talented; they knew a lot about music and how to make good music. But they did not do it alone. They all had teams of people—producers, managers, agents, writers, etc.—who helped them reach such incredible levels of success. The point is that even if you feel as though you have your retirement under control on your own, you might be missing out on some valuable insights that a trusted advisor could offer that might make a significant difference in your future success as a retiree.

Remember the puzzle analogy I gave earlier? What does the picture on the front of your retirement box look like? If you have not done it already, take some time to think about it and write down your goals:

- How do I want to spend my retirement?
- What is something I have always dreamed of doing but have not been able to because of work, family, and life's many other obligations?

Some of your goals might seem unattainable or unrealistic, but write them down anyway! Your advisor might be able to help you get there.

Once you have a trusted advisor on your side, get together and lay out the puzzle pieces you have so far that make up your picture of retirement. Discuss your picture of retirement. Your advisor will help you figure out where each piece goes, what is realistic for you, and if there are any changes you can make now regarding your assets, investments, and so on, to have a more successful retirement.

Finally, focus on the opportunities that await you, but do not overlook the lurking dangers that you might not realize exist. I am not telling you to have a doomsday plan for every possible negative thing that could happen, but you need to accept the fact that there is no fountain of youth. You will grow old, and your body will not work as well as it did years ago. You must plan for the inevitable: illness, injuries, old age frailty, finding a proper place to live if your current home no longer suits your needs, and the most inevitable of all—death. I always like to look at the positive side of things, but if you look at these events as a natural part of life, they become much less scary and negative, and you learn how to roll with the punches.

Quick Riffs:

- Find an advisor—visit danielsfinancialgroup.com to learn more about me, my practice, and our philosophies.
- Meet with your advisor—share your puzzle-box picture, lay out your puzzle pieces, and start putting the pieces together into a plan.
- Do not ignore the inevitable events you will encounter as you age—embrace them!

Playlist:

1. "Rock Around the Clock," Bill Haley & His Comets (1954)
2. "Time Has Come Today," The Chamber Brothers (1967)
3. "No Time," The Guess Who (1969)
4. "Time," Pink Floyd (1973)
5. "Time is on My Side," The Rolling Stones (1964)
6. "Time in a Bottle," Jim Croce (1972)
7. "Time Won't Let Me," The Outsiders (1965)
8. "Turn! Turn! Turn! (To Everything There Is a Season)," The Byrds (1965)
9. "Cat's in the Cradle," Harry Chapin (1974)
10. "Old Man," Neil Young (1972)
11. "Haven't Got Time for the Pain," Carly Simon (1974)
12. "Time" Pozo-Seko Singers (1965)
13. "Funny How Time Slips Away," Willie Nelson (1962)
14. "Blue Hawaii," Elvis Presley (1961)
15. "Centerfield," John Fogerty (1985)
16. "Let's Live for Today," The Grass Roots (1971)

CHAPTER 2:

Money (That's What I Want)

Money don't get everything, it's true. But what it don't get,

I can't use. I need money (that's what I want).

—*"Money (That's What I Want)," Barrett Strong (1959)*

Love (or lack thereof) is probably the number-one subject of classic rock's greatest hits. However, I would say the subject of money has got to be in the top ten. "The best things in life are free, but you can give them to the birds and bees . . . " You know the rest of the lyrics; multiple classic-rock bands covered this song, originally a Motown hit in the late 1950s.

And Paul McCartney may have been right when he wrote, "I don't care too much for money, money can't buy me love," but you know what money can buy: airplane tickets, vacations, lake houses, boats, fun stuff with the grandkids, and anything else you envision owning or doing once you're retired. Not to mention basic living expenses.

Of course, you know what money does. If I were to ask a dozen clients what money does, they would all be able to answer, and the answers would all likely be similar. But if I asked a dozen clients to write down what they think money *is*, the answers would be all over the place.

Simply defined, money is the circulating medium of exchange as defined by a government. You *exchange it* for goods or services. You might say that money is the blood that flows through the world's economy.

Why is this important? People with an understanding of what money *is*—its uses and misuses—are far more successful at putting it to good use than those who only think about what it *does*. Acquiring a reasonable understanding of what money is can help you use it wisely and improve your chances for a successful outcome. Hopefully, by the end of this book, you will feel more confident in your understanding of how to use it.

A Dollar Down and a Dollar a Week

Just a dollar down and a dollar a week, you can get all the things you seek, for a dollar down and a dollar a week.
—*"A Dollar Down," The Limeliters (1961)*

In 1961, the Limeliters charted with a spruced-up version of an old Woody Guthrie tune, "A Dollar Down." This has to be the best tune I've ever heard on the consequences of misusing credit. It's the tale of a poor fellow, and later his wife, who eventually end up over their heads in debt. Take a listen with your kids and grandkids, and then remind them—and yourself—to take heed to the final verse:

As their debts began to mount,
They added them up upon a sheet.
They said with tears, we'll take a thousand years
at a dollar down and a dollar a week.

There are few things we can get today for a dollar a week, but even though money itself hasn't changed over the years, the way we think about it and use it has come a long way.

When I was growing up, you spent what you had. Credit was reserved only for major purchases, like a house or a car. When we went out for dinner, bought new clothes, or went grocery shopping, we didn't use credit. Cash was king. Now we are heading into a paperless society where credit is king instead. The mind-set is different now—charge now, pay later. I do not want to make credit sound like an indictment of our society today, because it has its positive uses—but it is certainly a foible of many people and leads to long-term consequences.

There are two different money phases we go through in life: one where we're actively trying to gather our wealth and the other where we need to slow things down. That active phase is the accumulation phase. This is when you are working to meet all of your essential expenses—food, clothing, and housing for yourself and your family. If you can afford it, you have lifestyle expenses, one of which is hopefully putting a little bit of money away for later. During this phase, you're building "tall" money.

Once you retire, accumulation should not be the driving force. Now you're in the distribution phase of your life when you want to create "long" money, otherwise known as lifetime income streams.

Two of the dangers that people face in retirement are:

- running out of money
- unknown health-care costs

There is risk involved during the accumulation phase, but not all risk is bad, especially when you're investing for the long haul; it's what makes an investment an investment. But when you reach the distribution phase, I would caution anyone against relying too much on investments for their income. Timing is everything, and siphoning money away from your investments during a period of market decline can cause your retirement assets to become depleted beyond repair.

Take the following, for example:

If you take a 5 percent distribution from an investment correlated with the stock market, and if the market suffers a 10 percent decline, then you aren't just down that 10 percent—you're down 15 percent total. Then, even if the market comes back up 15 percent the following year, it's only adding 15 percent to what you have left in that investment, so your investment is still down. If the market continues to decline for multiple years, and if you continue to deplete your core investment amount by taking annual distributions from it, then there may be dire consequences later on.

Instead, the long money of the distribution phase should be managed with products specifically designed for guaranteed lifetime income to create funds for your retirement income base. Remaining assets can comfortably stay invested for years, possibly decades, without the fear of your income being affected negatively by market swings.

In the late sixties, there was a group that played in my hometown of Lorain, Ohio, that used to "slow things down" at the old Lincoln Park Ballroom with the Gerry and the Pacemakers tune "Don't Let the Sun Catch You Crying." The guy doing vocals always managed to replace the word "crying" with "trying." The first time I heard it, being young and dumb, I asked the girl sitting next to me, "Trying what?" She whispered the answer in my ear. I responded with blushing cheeks, "Oh yeah, I knew that!"

I don't want any of my clients to wake up after a bad period in the market and have "the sun catch them crying"; that's why it is best to start thinking about the distribution phase when you are still in the accumulation phase—the earlier, the better. I encourage you to think of retirement in the same way you would think of running a business (or starting a successful rock band!); one of the first things a successful business does is create a budget. They look at what their expenses are going to be, and they match those expenses with their projected income.

And even if you plan to not bring in any income for a while, like the Grateful Dead did when they played free concerts early on in their career, you should budget now not only for when you do start to show a profit but also for what your projected retirement income needs will be during a retirement that could last twenty years or more.

During my interview process, I ask people if they think that adhering to a budget is a good idea. Usually I get a resounding yes. But when I ask if they actually have a budget to adhere to, surprisingly I get many noes. In today's world of media glitz, there seems to be an overabundance of information on how to best align your investments for retirement. Some I agree with; some, in my opinion, might be a bit over the top. Call me plain-vanilla Danny if you want to, but if I work with you in an advisory capacity, one of the first things we are going to do is develop a reasonable retirement budget for you. Because when you retire, you will be on a fixed income, and people on a fixed income simply can't spend more than they make! When a business outspends its income, it will eventually go out of business. That's just common sense. The same thing can happen in retirement if you're not careful. I know that there's no "glitz" in planning a budget and that it takes work to adhere to one. But for retirees—particularly those with limited assets—it's the cornerstone of a long-term plan.

Sit down with your advisor and look at your essential expenses and your lifestyle expenses. These change after you retire, and your advisor can help you determine how yours might change. It is different for everybody, depending on factors such as income level during the accumulation phase, current health issues, the nature of your job (such as physically demanding labor), the size of your family, the area you live in, and more.

Take some time to consider these and other factors that could affect your expenses during retirement. You will also want to consider the risks that are inherent to retirement and aging, which I will discuss in detail in chapter 3. And do not forget to factor in a reasonable inflation rate: 3 or 4 percent is an historical average.

Next, take a look at your guaranteed income sources. While certain income streams may come and go, we can still assume that things like Social Security will still be guaranteed in our retirement, as would a pension from work. Your advisor can help you compare your expenses with your income sources. In my experience, most clients have greater expenses than they do income after retirement. They may have enough money in their savings to dip into for five to ten years, but what about after? Eventually, investments might dwindle down, even disappear, and in the tenth or fifteenth year, they may end up crashing and burning because they're at a point in their lives when they're not able to go back to work and refill those investment buckets.

Consider famous singer-songwriter Willie Nelson and his run-in with the IRS in 1990. Caught for failing to pay close to $17 million in back taxes, Willie, then age fifty-seven, filed for bankruptcy. A short time later, he released the album *The IRS Tapes: Who'll Buy My Memories?*—the entire proceeds from which went right to the IRS. Fortunately for Willie, he was still able to crank out the tunes to pay for his lack of planning, but that's rarely the case for many of us who, by our early sixties, often have few or no options to generate extra income streams.

Even if you can't sing your way out of debt, there may be distribution methods available that you do not even know about. Perhaps you have investments that you plan on using as income during retirement. However, are you confident that those investments were made to become an income-producing source? I will talk more about different types of investments in chapter 6, but this is an ideal question to bring to your advisor if you're not confident of the answer.

The good news is that an experienced advisor can guide you and help you look forward so you have some idea of what your retirement is going to look like.

The advantages are not only financial but psychological as well. With an advisor on your team, you may feel more confident going forward, knowing that there may be economic calamities, market ups and downs, and health events that you have no way of preventing. An advisor-led plan considers all of these things so you can be prepared.

Quick Riffs:

What factors may affect your expenses during retirement? Having answers ready to the following questions will help you and your advisor more accurately design your long-term retirement plans:

- How is your current health? Do you have any chronic conditions? Conditions that are known to worsen with age? What about your spouse? Do you have any dependents?
- What is your family's health history? Should you anticipate the possibility of inheriting a genetic condition? Is there longevity in your family?
- Where do you live? What is the weather like, and how does it affect your lifestyle and your expenses? What kind of house and/ or land do you own? How does the upkeep affect your budget?
- What are some of your goals for retirement?
- If your parents are still living, what is their living situation like? Are you a caregiver, or could you become one in the future?
- Before you retire you work for your money.
  During retirement your money works for you.
  Plan accordingly!

Playlist:

1. "Money," Pink Floyd (1973)
2. "Mercedes Benz," Janis Joplin (1970)
3. "Money (That's What I Want)," Barrett Strong (1959)
4. "Baby, You're a Rich Man," The Beatles (1967)
5. "Money, Money," The Grateful Dead (1974)
6. "Danny's Song," Loggins & Messina (1971)
7. "Can't Buy Me Love," The Beatles (1964)
8. "Rich Girl," Hall & Oates (1977)
9. "Take the Money and Run," The Steve Miller Band (1976)
10. "Don't Let the Sun Catch You Crying," Jerry and the Pacemakers (1964)
11. "A Dollar Down," The Limeliters (1961)
12. "Pay You Back with Interest," The Hollies (1967)

CHAPTER 3:

For What It's Worth:
Five Types of Financial Risks
We're All Likely to Run Into

We better stop—hey, what's that sound? Everybody, look—what's going down?
— *"For What It's Worth," Buffalo Springfield, (1966)*

When the Kinks first recorded their famous tune "You Really Got Me," band member Ray Davies insisted that the recording done by their studio label was too slow and overproduced. Despite the record label refusing to pay for another recording session, Davies was able to convince producer Shel Talmy to underwrite another recording session, and the edgy classic-rock song with its memorable distorted guitar riff was born. For Ray Davies, it was a risk standing up to the only record label that would agree to sign them at the time (several labels turned them down before Pye Records signed them in 1964), but the results were incredible: number one on the UK charts and top ten in the US in less than two months.[1]

Risks, as we all know, are a part of life, and no one is immune to them. But the more we know about risks as we approach them, the better we tend to come out on the other side.

There are the usual risks that most people talk about, such as investments, the stock market, and the economy, as well as market risk, inflation risk, and tax risk. All of these are legitimate topics to discuss with your advisor, but in this chapter, my goal is to share with you the five different types of financial risks that you don't often hear others talk about—the reality risks that happen in life if you live long enough.

Risk #1: Procrastination Risk

It's your life and you can do what you want, do what
you like, but please don't keep me waiting
—*"Tired of Waiting for You," The Kinks (1965)*

When I first joined Mutual of Omaha more than thirty-five years ago, it was just me and my wife. We lived in a nice mobile-home court in northeast Ohio, and I was working long hours. Oftentimes, on my way home, I would pick up my wife at her parent's home, and we would stop at a little tavern on Lake Erie. For about two years, we did this. The tavern was run by a nice fellow, and his wife and son worked there with him. It was a great place to unwind after work and enjoy a good burger, a cold beer, and some rock tunes on the jukebox.

I often thought about approaching the owner and telling him about what I do—maybe he could use some help with acquiring life insurance or

---

1   "The Kinks," Wikipedia, https://en.wikipedia.org/wiki/The_Kinks

something else. But I never did. I kept putting it off because I was afraid he would think wrong of me, that I was some kind of pushy insurance guy. Perhaps I was afraid of rejection, too.

After my wife and I moved about thirty miles away, we stopped going to the tavern. Then, about a year after we moved, the son of the owner came into my Mutual of Omaha office looking for a job. I remembered him right away.

"Aren't you the young fella who used to work at that tavern?" He confirmed he was. "How are your mom and dad doing?" I asked.

"Didn't you know? Dad passed away. He had a massive heart attack and died. Mom lost the business," he said. "I'm out of work, looking for a job."

He told me that his dad did not have life insurance or any kind of business-succession plan in place for this kind of unexpected event. His mom could not do it on her own, so she lost the place. But what she did not lose was the debt that she and her husband incurred to start the business.

I offered my belated condolences. I am not sure how you respond to something like that. All I could think of was how much I regretted the fact that in all the times my wife and I went in there, I never approached the fellow and said, "By the way, I'm Danny Smith. I work for Mutual of Omaha Insurance. Maybe I can help you plan. Let's sit down and talk a little bit, I'd like to tell you how I work with small business owners." What would have been the worst that could have happened? He could have said, "No thanks, Danny, not right now." But what if he had said yes? I couldn't have prevented him from having a heart attack and dying, but I could have helped him get an affordable amount of life insurance. Then maybe his family could have been protected financially and the restaurant saved.

We both made the major mistake of procrastinating and not taking action: I didn't talk to him when I could have, and he didn't consider the fact that his family would be left with nothing should he pass away suddenly. When he died, his family lost everything and found themselves in significant debt.

Because as much as any bank employee might like to say, "I'm sorry about your husband's death. Just forget about the loan," it's not going to happen. As my good friend and noted attorney Jim Aussem says, "there is no substitute for cash when a small business owner dies. Life insurance is often the best and most affordable way to do this."

To this day, I do not know what happened to the widow. All I know is that the business closed and never reopened.

I wish I could say his story was unique. Never getting started on your life insurance in the first place can have dramatic effects on your retirement. Often when I am meeting with people, I explain to them the logic of planning, what they can do with what they have, what they need to do, and so forth. They answer, "Okay, well, I want to think about it."

"Think about what?" I reply. "Do you want to think about the next thirty years of a successful retirement and doing the things necessary to have the highest probability of that happening? What is there to think about?"

Usually, that grabs their attention.

As an advisor, one of my jobs is to give people a gentle nudge—or sometimes a swift kick—to get them started. If you never do anything, if you keep putting it off and saying you will start next year and then never do . . . well, there is a heavy price to pay for that. Some people find it daunting, understandably, but getting started is nowhere near as scary as going into retirement without a plan.

My Poem about Procrastination

I knew I should

I said I would

But I didn't

Risk #2: Longevity Risk

Will you still need me, will you still feed me . . .
—*"When I'm Sixty-Four," The Beatles (1967)*

The best way I can explain longevity risk is to tell you about my wife's great-uncle, Pete. I remember him as a cantankerous, old guy with a firm handshake and bright smile. He immigrated to the United States from Croatia sometime in the 1930s. He spoke broken English and always kept a bottle of whiskey nearby, even when he was in the nursing home. As was his custom, he expected every visitor to drink a shot with him before the conversation got started because that was how they did it in the old days.

Uncle Pete's goal in life was to leave something behind to his family members, many of which still lived in Croatia. Unfortunately, as is often the case with older people, the last years of his life were fraught with health decline, and he ended up in the nursing home. By the time he passed away, what he considered his fortune to be left behind—over $100,000—had been used up to pay for his care. I remember vividly how his niece Anna, who was also his guardian, would sit in my office and weep as his assets dwindled to pay for his care. She and I both knew that Uncle Pete's dream to leave something behind was going up in smoke. When he would inquire about his money, Anna and I always assured him that he was doing fine. I guess that's the right thing to do for a person in his situation, but in reality, it broke both of our hearts to know what was really happening.

Uncle Pete has been gone for many years, yet his story remains with me. It is not one that you forget! As I mentioned earlier, I love my job and like to have fun doing it, but as any veteran advisor will tell you: it's impossible to do this job without sharing in the emotions of the people we serve. Sometimes that means laughter, and sometimes it means holding someone's hand to assure them that everything is going to be okay or shedding a tear with the family of someone who has died. I am not ashamed to say that I am very grateful that God has granted me the ability to do that.

Uncle Pete ended up living a lot longer than anyone anticipated. His story is a perfect example of longevity risk. By the time he passed away, most of what he wanted to leave behind was dissipated, spent on nursing-home and health-care costs.

The fact is that you are more than likely going to live a long time after you retire. Look at the statistics. Men retiring at age sixty-five now have a 40 percent chance of reaching age eighty-five, and women retiring at sixty-five have an even greater chance—53 percent—of reaching eighty-five. Take healthy living into account, and those same chances increase to 50 percent for men and 62 percent for women.[2] Couples have a longer life expectancy than individuals. A married person has a greater than 50 percent chance of living to age ninety-two or ninety-three.

This is not a bad thing—who doesn't want to live a long and fruitful life? Right? But too few people take the time to plan for that. Why that is, I do not know. The longer you live, the more good things you can do in your life, but the chances of running into a bump in the road or a pothole or even a minefield grow as well. Your advisor can show you some scenarios regarding what to expect and how many successful years of retirement you currently have. Then he or she can address the dangers that might cause that scenario to crash and burn. Although there are no perfect solutions to longevity risk, proactive planning is probably the best way to manage it and prevent what happened to Uncle Pete from happening to you.

---

2   "Key Findings and Issues: Longevity—2011 Risks and Process of Retirement Survey Report," Society of Actuaries, June 2012.

Risk #3: Decisional Risk

People runnin' everywhere, don't know the way to go.
Don't know where I am, can't see past the next step,
don't have to think past the last mile.
—*"Does Anybody Really Know What Time It Is?" Chicago (1969)*

Before they settled on the name "Chicago" in the 1970s, Chicago was first known by the rather generic name the Big Thing. Then, for a brief time, they were known as the Chicago Transit Authority until the real Chicago Transit Authority took issue with it and started legal proceedings against the band. Who knows if Chicago would have reached the level of notoriety that they've enjoyed from the 1970s up to today if they'd stuck with "The Big Thing"—but my gut feeling is that they might not have been known for much of anything, big or otherwise.

Changing their name was a risk, but it was one that definitely worked in their favor. When it comes to finances, decisions can be made based on the extensive knowledge of your experienced, certified, and well-intentioned financial advisor, but you want to avoid basing them on bad advice. These are what we call "decisional risks," or risks you take when you base your financial decisions on bad advice from someone who does not know what he or she is talking about.

We have all made poor decisions at some point in our lives based on someone else's incorrect and/or irrelevant information. For example, you may have heard of the term "Dr. Google." With access to so much information on the Internet, it is not uncommon for people to make medical decisions based on something they read online. However, if your doctor gave you some advice, such as to have a surgery that could save your life or significantly improve your health, what would you do? You might get a second opinion from another doctor, but hopefully you would not pass on the surgery because of some random online article claiming that you could cure your disease with omega-3 and some B vitamins.

Unfortunately, when it comes to making financial and retirement decisions, I hear statements like this all the time. I ask a client, "Why did you do that?" and he answers, "Well, because the guy I work with told me that's what he did," or "Well, my uncle was a financial advisor for a short time, and he said you're all wrong." At which point I inquire, "What's he doing now?" and they answer, "Oh, he's on unemployment."

This is why it is vital to find an advisor who has a proven track record of competency and trustworthiness. Find someone who can help you make the right decisions or at least give you a higher probability of success. Advisors can't predict the future. Even the best surgeons in the world will tell you that the worst outcome possible when undergoing surgery is that you won't wake up, but there is a higher probability of living a long and fruitful life if you go through with it than if you do not.

Risk #4: Generational Risk

But I know sometimes I must get out of the light, better
leave her behind with the kids, the kids are alright.
—*"The Kids Are Alright," The Who (1965)*

When guitarist legend Jimi Hendrix died in 1970 at the incredibly young age of twenty-seven, he left no will behind and, consequently, his family was arguing over his financial estate as recently as 2004.[3] This lack of planning—and even though Hendrix was young, his personal wealth was

---

3   Brian Alexander, "Judge Settles Long Family Feud Over Jimi Hendrix's Estate," Sep. 25, 2004, http://www.nytimes.com/2004/09/25/us/judge-settles-long-family-feud-over-jimi-hendrixs-estate.html?_r=0.

such that he should have at least had a basic plan in place—is what I would call a "generational risk."

Regardless of whether you're a young adult or aging gracefully, generational risk is how the consequences of improper planning negatively affects the generation you leave behind. If you have assets and you pass away tomorrow, your family will be left with your money. On one hand, that is good, but on the other hand, if you leave them money but with no plan or instructions, many problems could arise. The last thing you want to have happen when you die is for the fortune you left behind to cause division and strife amongst your family. History is full of millions and billions of dollars that have been inherited and then squandered away or fought over by siblings, children, and spouses of the deceased. In truth, I could easily write an entire book about the unintended consequences of poor generational planning or no planning. I would probably title it *Fortunes Lost* or maybe *How Mom and Dad's Money Screwed Up My Life.*

In my firm, we have a process that can help you determine if you might experience generational risk. From your perspective, you might not see any at all—no one wants to believe that their children or spouses would fight over money. But loving, closely knit families all throughout history have wound up torn apart in estate battles. And these situations don't just happen after death; they can happen during your lifetime as well. Working with an attorney who is schooled in this area to obtain properly planned legal documents and organizing your assets with your advisor are among things you can do to minimize generational risk.

You cannot prevent your loved ones from making bad decisions after your die. But leaving them with a well-planned estate will surely save them a lot of conflict and heartache.

Risk #5: Catastrophe Health-Care Planning: The Risk of the Great Unknown

Well, I saw the thing coming out of the sky. It had one long
horn and one big eye. I commenced to shakin' and I said,
"Oo-ee, it looks like a Purple People Eater to me."
—*"The Purple People Eater," Sheb Wooley (1958)*

The longer you live, the greater the risk there is of experiencing an unplanned health-care event. A longer life also means you are more likely to move into an assisted-living facility or nursing home. In Ohio, where I live, annual nursing-home expenses average about $85,000. The cost varies in each state, however, with Alaska having the highest nursing-home costs as of 2015 at about $280,000 per year.[4] And that's only if you get in. Most assisted-living facilities have a waiting list that ranges from several months to several years. At Menorah Park in the Cleveland neighborhood of Beachwood, Ohio, the waiting list can run in excess of two years! In spite of this, the most-asked question about assisted-living facilities is not "Can we get in?" but "Can we afford to get in?" Having a trusted advisor by your side to help you with major decisions like this can be comforting when dealing with so many oft-unconsidered aspects of planning the rest of your life.

One way I like to explain this longevity risk to my fellow baby-boomer clients is by referring to those science-fiction movies we all watched in the 1950s, such as *The Thing from Another World* and *Earth vs. The Flying Saucers*. Those gorgeous black and white pictures, with the flying saucers and the aliens who were always far ahead of us earthlings in terms of technology, were thrilling to watch despite their often-similar plot lines. In many cases,

---

4   "Nursing Home Costs," Skilled Nursing Facilities, http://www.skillednurs-ingfacilities.org/resources/nursing-home-costs/

the aliens would use their technology to wreak havoc on Earth, leaving us scrambling to save mankind. Then, in the last ten minutes of the movie, the scientists on Earth would all get together and create some sort of gadget, like a ray gun, to send the aliens on their way. Wouldn't it have been easier if the scientists had a plan for such an unknown risk? Fortunately, in those movies, mankind almost, but not always, wins. Check out those darn pods in *The Invasion of the Body Snatchers* to see what I mean.

If you're in the last "reel" of your life, have little or no planning, and unexpected "aliens" (i.e., health-care issues and costs) show up on your doorstep, it is most likely too late to create that new ray gun to save you. The most difficult time to try to make decisions is when you're under duress.

We have to take into consideration the risk of the great unknown—longevity—just in case aliens land on our porch. You need to have *something* planned. You may be asking, "What exactly do I need?" But before you can answer that, you first need to determine your risks. Even the best financial-retirement planning won't prevent the unavoidable health events associated with aging, but a well-thought-out and structured plan can help avoid financial loss or ruin due to catastrophic health events.

Quick Riffs:

What kinds of risks are you open to as you approach retirement?

- Take a moment to list all the happy things you want to have happen during your life and in your retirement. Ask yourself if you have the optimum plan to allow you to do all those things.
- Now list all of the things that you think could happen that would cause those plans to crash and burn in a moment's notice. Ask yourself if you have done all you possibly can to mitigate those risks.

What are the risks inherent to your lifestyle? Your answers to the questions in chapter 2 can help you determine risks related to your home, health, and family history. Also think about what kind of risks you face based on:

- Your job: Does it risk your physical safety? Your mental health? Does it involve potential legal issues? Do you travel a lot?
- Your hobbies: Are you an adrenaline junkie? Do you have any expensive hobbies or collect expensive items?
- Your financial habits: Do you make risky financial decisions?

Once you are finished, your advisor can help you create a plan that optimizes your opportunities for all of those good things and also allows you to minimize the impact when those bad things happen. When you have a plan that addresses both, you'll have the peace of mind and the satisfaction of knowing that you've done as much as possible to allow yourself a carefree, happy retirement. If there's a bend in the river or a bump in the road, your plan is optimized to minimize the risks and dangers that it could cause. That's the power of having a plan.

Playlist:

1. "The Flying Saucer Parts 1 & 2," Buchanan & Goodman (1955)
2. "The Purple People Eater," Sheb Wooley (1958)
3. "Frankenstein," Edgar Winter Group (1973)
4. "Godzilla," Blue Oyster Cult (1977)
5. "Werewolves of London," Warren Zevon (1978)
6. "I've Seen All Good People," Yes (1971)
7. "Another Brick in the Wall," Pink Floyd (1979)
8. "Gimme Me Three Steps," Lynyrd Skynyrd (1973)

9. "You Can't Always Get What You Want"
   The Rolling Stones (1969)

10. "For What It's Worth," Buffalo Springfield (1966)

11. "Tired of Waiting for You," The Kinks (1965)

12. "Does Anybody Really Know What Time It Is?"
    Chicago (1969)

13. "The Kids Are Alright," The Who (1965)

Watchlist – 1950s Movies:

1. *Creature from the Black Lagoon* (1954)

2. *The Day the Earth Stood Still* (1951)

3. *The Thing from Another World* (1951)

4. *Them!* (1954)

5. *Invasion of the Body Snatchers* (1956)

6. *I Was a Teenage Werewolf* (1957)

7. *Godzilla* (1954)

8. *Tarantula* (1955)

9. *Plan 9 from Outer Space* (1959) . . .
   (Arguably the worst movie ever made.)

10. *Robot Monster* (1953) . . . (So bad it's good!
    And dig those rabbit ears and bubble machine!)

CHAPTER 4:

It's My Life (Insurance)

It's my life and I'll do what I want, it's my mind and I'll think what I want.
Show me I'm wrong, hurt me some time, but some day I'll treat you real fine.
—*"It's My Life," The Animals (1965)*

Early in my career, when I didn't have the client base I have today, I would make the rounds every December to visit as many of my clients as possible and give them a Mutual of Omaha *Wild Kingdom* calendar—a beautiful, utilitarian calendar that they still make today.

Two of those clients—Jim and Nancy—lived in a suburb of Cleveland, Ohio, and every year I looked forward to visiting them because they were always kind, and I was always welcomed.

On this particular visit, after talking with Jim for a while, he said, "Danny, I've been a police officer for thirty years, and I'm going to retire. I'm wondering what your thoughts are."

"Well, Jim," I replied, "Have you evaluated your benefits? Do you know what's going to happen to them?"

He explained that he would be able to keep his health insurance but that his life insurance would be gone once he retired. He said, "Our kids are still young; I want to make sure they're financially protected if something happens to me."

I suggested he take some of the money he had been contributing to his IRA and use it toward permanent life insurance.

"Danny, that's a great idea," he said. "But a few years back, I had a bout with leukoplakia, a type of oral cancer. I don't think I can get life insurance."

During that period in my career, I was fortunate to have been befriended and mentored by one of Mutual of Omaha's top agents at that time, Alvin Horwitz. I wish I had more space in my book to tell you about "Al." All I can say is that there are precious few "one-in-a-million people" in this world, but Al was definitely one of them. He taught me that, no matter what, if you think there's a chance to get life insurance for a client, then you should try. The worst outcome would be for the insurance company to decline the application.

So I suggested to Jim that I submit a nonbinding application on his behalf and have him go through the normal underwriting process. He agreed. To my surprise, Mutual of Omaha made an offer for a $250,000 policy, which Jim gladly accepted.

About five months after that, Jim gave me a call. "Danny," he said, "the cancer has come back. I'm not sure what the outcome will be, so I just want to make sure my life insurance policy is okay."

I assured Jim that his policy was fine, and he said he would keep me informed.

The day after New Year's Day, I was in the office when the phone rang. Lily, the office manager at that time, was calling to let me know that Nancy was on the phone. To this day I remember putting my hand on the receiver and having an immediate premonition. I knew that Nancy was calling to tell me that Jim had died. I had no way of knowing that, but I did.

"Danny," Nancy said when I finally picked up the phone, "Jim passed away over the holidays, and I need you to come out to the house."

After Jim's funeral, I assisted Nancy in filing a claim with Mutual of Omaha and, as all good insurance companies do, they paid that claim to Nancy for $250,000, which allowed her to stay in her house and raise her children. It took a lot of pressure off of her financially.

To help supplement the family's income, Nancy used a portion of Jim's life insurance to purchase a type of annuity that pays an immediate income for a guaranteed period of time. To this day, she continues to receive a monthly stipend to help with expenses. As Nancy puts it, "I'm living off my life insurance." That money is still safely set aside, providing her with income even though Jim has been gone for so many years.

Jim and Nancy's story has stayed with me my whole career, and I still call on Nancy from time to time. Despite the years, even as I recount this story for you, the emotion I felt that day is still as fresh as ever. It was a sad series of events, but I am glad that I could be a part of it and help that family minimize the financial impact of Jim's death.

As I quoted the Animals' lead singer Eric Burdon at the beginning of this chapter, ". . . someday I'll treat you real fine," one of the finest things that Jim did for Nancy and his family before he died was to purchase life insurance.

Free Copy of Nancy's Story

My friends at Mutual of Omaha have produced a beautifully done DVD called *Nancy's Story* featuring Nancy and her daughter, which I would love to share with you. To request your own copy, send an email to danny.dfg@adviserfocus.com or call 1-800-783-2061 and let us know that you'd like a complimentary copy of *Nancy's Story*.

What's Insurance Got to Do with It?

You may be wondering why I am dedicating a part of my book to insurance when it's supposed to help people plan for retirement. Here's why. One of the surest ways to have your retirement plan crash and burn is to suffer a catastrophic health event or die before you get to retirement. If your employer offers a pension, its official name is a defined benefit plan. That's because the eventual payout is "defined" by a formula that includes years of service and maximum income years, which are usually your last years of employment. Social Security uses a similar formula. If you are self-employed and have to fund your own retirement plan, where will the money come from if you can't open the doors and earn an income? The ripple effect of a disability, particularly as you approach retirement, can be dramatic if not devastating. And death, investable as it is, almost always carries a price tag. Similarly, a large causality claim can wreak havoc on finances and your future regardless of when it might happen. Then there are postretirement health-care issues that might have to be dealt with through insurance.

I remind you that insurance, any type of insurance, does not prevent bad things from happening. Insurance does not eliminate the risks we face in life, however, it can cushion financial consequences if and when that proverbial big, bad, wolf knocks on our door. An advisor's job is to evaluate client's risks then provide reasonable solutions. Sometimes—but not always—an insurance solution is the best way to go. I remind you that while not everyone needs the same types of insurance, everyone needs a plan that addresses the risks that we face in life.

What's Your Life Worth?

"And if you're downright disgusted, and your life ain't worth a dime, get a girl with far away eyes."
—*"Far Away Eyes," The Rolling Stones (1978)*

In all my years in the business, it never ceases to amaze me how we as human beings are more than willing to insure the replaceable things we own to full value. You want your house and autos insured to their estimated replacement costs, right? But the one thing that *is not* replaceable—life— we sometimes insure for far less than its value. Every life is irreplaceable, and everyone's life is worth far more than the proverbial *dime* that Mick and Keith refer to. But how much is your life really worth? How do you put a price tag on life for insurance purposes?

We insure the "things" we own based on a reasonable estimate of their value. But life insurance is not about replacing "things." It's about providing money so the *things that we will do in life if we live will get done in case we die*: things like paying off the mortgage and other debts, the financial security of our family, our kid's education, and maybe keeping the lights on at the business. In later years, life insurance provides financial protection for your spouse or partner from the uncertainties of life without you and possibly leaving something behind to help others less fortunate.

When I counsel people about life insurance, I show them the Lifetime Income Calculator *(see page 63)* and ask, "Have you ever thought about the fortune you'll earn if you live and keep your health?" Then I have them do the calculation. If that person makes $100,000 annually for the next twenty years, he or she will earn over $2 million. I have them write that figure on a legal pad, and then I ask, "How much of that amount do you want to protect if something happens to you?" Not everyone is able to do the full amount, but few respond, "Well, none of it." Life is precious!

But there is an intangible side of life, and living that is much harder to value in dollars. It really has nothing to do with life insurance. I mention it because it will give you a better idea of how I think and hopefully something for you to think about. Over the course of our lives, we have all come in contact with people who in one way or another helped us become the people we are today. The list could include parents, grandparents, teachers, coaches, teammates, writers, people we've worked for or with, etc. I call these people *difference makers*. How do you affix a value on the love of a parent and spouse, the education from that special teacher, the encouragement of a coach, or the stewardship of a mentor? But what if that *difference maker* died before he or she came into your life? Could your life have possibly turned out differently? I am here to say that mine would have. Were it not for the intervention that I received from some caring people many years ago, God only knows where I could have ended up. Perhaps some of you have similar stories. The classic holiday movie *It's a Wonderful Life* has got to be the best example I can think of about what happens when a difference maker—in this case Jimmy Stewart's character—dies an untimely death. I will never be able to fully repay the difference makers in my life nor can I possibly affix a dollar value to their intervention. However, I do try to be a positive influence on the younger people that I meet, hoping that in some small measure to replenish the help that was given to me and if possible be a difference maker too!

Composing Your Ideal Life Insurance Plan

When composing music, regardless of whether it's classical or classic rock, one tends to start with a basic melody and build around it. Keith Richards says that the melody for "Satisfaction" came to him in the middle of the night, and he built it into one of the most recognized rock songs of all time.

The same construct goes for life insurance: you start with the basic foundation—call it a needs analysis. Think of it as an appraisal of the economic engine called "you," and you build around it until it sounds just right.

When people ask me, "What's the best type of life insurance policy?" my answer is always the same: "It's the one that's in force the day you die."

Since this book is more of a "quick-start" guide rather than a detailed textbook on financial planning, I'll forego the details and just say that, essentially, there are two types of life insurance: permanent and term. An easy way to understand the difference between the two is to think of it as *purchasing* a car versus *leasing* a car. When you purchase a car, you can pay cash for it or take out a loan and make a payment each month. Eventually, you end up owning the car; it's yours to keep and it counts as an asset, which is its value. This is similar to the cash accumulation within a permanent life insurance policy.

When you lease a car, you pay a lower payment every month, but at the end of the lease cycle, you give the car back or purchase it outright per the terms of the lease. Term insurance works in a similar fashion.

Which is the right way to go? It depends on what is the best pathway for each individual. Similar to automobiles, sometimes it is better to buy, and sometimes it is better to lease.

In many cases, term life insurance can be affordable with a low-cost premium, and you pay that premium until the term, or the "lease," is up. However, at this point, the policy doesn't actually terminate; rather, the premium begins to escalate—usually every year. The caution here is that your premiums could eventually become cost prohibitive in the later years. That's why most term polices allow you to "convert" some or all of the policy's death benefit to permanent coverage later on if it makes sense to do so. Term life insurance can be the best solution when the objective is to purchase the biggest death benefit at an affordable cost for a certain number of years. For example, young families on a budget may benefit from this type of policy.

Permanent life insurance can be an important component of a well-rounded, balanced financial strategy and a flexible asset to help you achieve your long-term goals. When structured properly, permanent life insurance offers:

- a death benefit, typically tax free, providing an efficient means to transfer wealth.
- tax-deferred growth of cash accumulation values
- an option of tax-favored distributions from cash accumulation value, giving you more spendable income.
- A properly structured permanent life insurance policy can provide safety, liquidity, protection, and important tax advantages that no other financial vehicle can offer in one package.

Note: Death benefit proceeds from a life insurance policy are generally not included in the gross income of the taxpayer/beneficiary. (Internal Revenue

Code Section 101(a)(1)). There are certain exceptions to this general rule including policies transferred for valuable consideration (IRC 101(a)(2)). Loans and withdrawals will decrease the cash value and death benefit. This information should not be construed as tax or legal advice. Consult with your tax or legal professional for details and guidelines specific to your situation.

One of the most common questions I'm asked is, "How much life insurance do I need?"

Well, how much are you worth?

Referring again to the chart on page 63, if you make $100,000 annually and you expect to work twenty more years, you are going to earn $2 million, even if you never get a raise. How much of that potential income do you think you should protect against the uncertainty that life brings every day?

Another Man Done Gone

Here's one point that I can't overemphasize; *in many cases, life insurance plays an integral role for women in retirement planning.* Why? According to the Census Bureau, 66.4 percent of women aged sixty-five or older are widowed.[5] And many of those widows could live five, ten, fifteen years past their spouse's death. There are those who believe in the conventional wisdom that says that, by the time you retire, your assets should be sufficient and you won't need life insurance anymore. I am not trying to lock horns with those who preach that theory, however, because *experience is my teacher and reality is my guide,* here is what I have found. During my interview process with couples, I always ask about the primary concern they each have about their futures. Responses are informative and often emotional. Based on my personal experience from hundreds of interviews, the wife's primary concern is usually worded as the

---

5   United States Census Bureau, *Marital Events of Americans: 2009,* issued August 2011, https://www.census.gov/prod/2011pubs/acs-13.pdf.

question, "What happens to me (financially) if something happens to him?" Having this question answered before something happens prevents a widow (or widower) from having to ask, "Now, what am I going to do?" I'm not saying that everyone going into retirement should include life insurance in his or her plan. However, not everyone goes into retirement completely debt-free with plenty of assets. And as the following story show, life's twists and turns can have unexpected consequences. Here's a cautionary and true story about what can happen when people make ill-advised financial decisions with life insurance. Logic might say that as people get older, they assume that they either don't need to purchase or no longer need their current life insurance, but that's not always the case.

This is the story of my friend, Lou, and his new bride, Betty Lu. When I was in my early twenties I worked in retail management with a company called Hills Department Stores. I met my friend Lou when we both worked at the Hills store in Horseheads, New York.

Although Lou was older than me, we became fast friends and as fate would have it, a few years after we met, Lou became the manager of the Hills store in my hometown Lorain, Ohio. I was assigned as his assistant manager, and we worked well together. Even after I left Hills, Lou and I remained friends.

Some years before I met Lou, he'd been through a nasty divorce and decided to let his life insurance policy lapse because he didn't think he needed it anymore. He never imagined that he would eventually get married again—and to a wonderful lady by the name of Betty Lu, who was about twenty years his junior. By that time I had left Hills and joined Mutual of Omaha. Knowing that I was in the insurance business, Lou asked me to come over and discuss life insurance with them.

As part of my training as a life insurance agent, I did some "fact-finding." I discovered that other than a small amount of group-term insurance through Lou's employment, he had no other life insurance. I also discovered that if Lou were to die, Betty Lu's income was nowhere near enough to pay the mortgage on their newly purchased home, her auto, and other debts they had incurred. Apparently they had not discussed life insurance before their marriage, because Betty Lu was shocked (and that's putting it mildly) when she realized the consequences that Lou's untimely death would have on her. Betty Lu asked me to give them a premium quote, which, for a guy Lou's age and with his health factors, came out at around $5,000 a year. I could tell right away that Lou did not want to pay that much. I think he was experiencing a case of sticker shock! I was right.

"Danny, come back later. Betty Lu and I have got to think about this," he said.

But Betty Lu stopped me right there.

"Danny, you're not going anywhere. Lou, do you mean to tell me that if you die, you don't have any life insurance? I'll lose this house, I'll lose the cars, I might lose everything?" she said. "Danny, you need to write up that application tonight!"

Any good life insurance salesperson will confirm that this was a positive sign! You just sit there, shut up, and let the aggrieved spouse close the sale for you. And that's exactly what happened.

Betty Lou determined (and eventually Lou agreed) that the pain of paying a $5,000 premium and sleeping on the couch was minuscule when compared to the financial consequences she would suffer if Lou died.

Every now and then, someone will call or come into the office and tell me that for whatever reason they're going to cancel their life insurance. It might be because of a divorce, the kids are grown, the house is paid for, or possibly one spouse or partner has died. Even though in my heart I believe it could be a bad decision on their part, I never try to talk them out of it or get upset. After all, I'm not the one paying the premium. I usually say something like, "Fine, if that's your decision, I'll assist to make sure that your wishes are honored. But before we do that, do you mind if I tell a you a couple of true stories that can help you decide?" If given the affirmative, I tell the stories of Jim and Nancy then Lou and Betty Lu. I don't do this because I'm concerned that the insurance company is going to lose a customer. I do it because I realize that sometimes we make short-term decisions, often based on the emotions of the moment, without considering their long-term consequences. If all I accomplish is to get people to think before they act—or as my mom used to say, "look before you leap"—I believe that I'm doing the right thing for those whom I serve.

In Lou's case, he would have been better off had he continued to fund the policies that he instead chose to cancel after his divorce. They were purchased when he was a younger and, indeed, a healthier man. Instead, he had to start over in his late fifties. Naturally, every person's case should be judged on its own merits, but policies purchased when you're younger and healthier should be carefully considered before cancelling them and then possibly having to start over again later in life.

The importance of this story is to remember that even if present circumstances lead you to believe that you no longer need life insurance, take a little time to think before you cancel it. We never know what life will bring or how our needs may change. Often in life, when one door closes a new door opens. For Lou and Betty Lu it was a happy door—theirs was a long and happy marriage. For Jim and Nancy, it was a sad door when Jim died of cancer soon after he retired. In both cases, life insurance was the most practical solution.

A family's financial strength and security may depend on a properly structured life insurance plan. This is especially true for younger families who have yet to build up an asset base. There is simply no substitute—no plan b. For younger families on a budget, inexpensive term life insurance can be a good solution. For a modest premium, younger folks can purchase a lot of term life insurance. Over the course of the policy's term, all or a part of it may be able to be converted to a permanent policy—if it makes sense to do so. The important thing is to have it in force if something happens. Also, starting out young with a term policy that is convertible with a guaranteed insurability rider protects future insurability should there be a health change that could affect a person's insurability or preclude them from qualifying at all. Parents and grandparents who want to give a *gift that lasts* after they're gone should consider rewarding a child or grandchild for graduating college or getting married by paying for what I call a starter policy. Oftentimes, permanent insurance such as whole life or some form of universal life can be used. Later on you can turn the policy over to them if you choose. For those who advocate that permanent life insurance isn't a good deal I have the following explanation: In my thirty-five-plus years in the insurance business I have worked with many people who had permanent "cash-value" polices purchased by parents (or grandparents). Not one of them has ever said, "Darn Mom and Dad for buying this policy on me!" But many have said that they wish Mom and Dad had done a few more things like this. In many instances, long after parents and grandparents are gone and the worldly gifts they made have been used up, the life insurance policy purchased perhaps decades ago remains as a testament to their love and foresight.

As I mentioned earlier, this book is a quick-start guide, not an in-depth instruction manual about insurance. That's why I'm not going into great detail on the various types of term and permanent polices that are currently available. To do so would be like trying to list all of the choices on the menu at a Chinese restaurant. There are times when term insurance is the best solution. Other times, a permanent insurance solution is best. Or perhaps a combination of the two is the way to go. A good advisor can sit down with you and evaluate your particular needs then design your life insurance program accordingly. That's different from someone trying to simply sell you a policy.

There are some in the financial-advice arena who advocate only owning term insurance. The belief is that when you're older you won't need life insurance because by then the kids are grown, college is out of the way, the house is paid for, and your investment buckets have grown large. I don't argue that, at times, a term solution is the right way to go. However, after more than thirty-five years in the insurance business I can say without hesitation that in many cases, older people—and I'm talking about us baby boomers—*do not* want to have their life insurance expire. That's because as we get older, we get wiser, and our belief systems change, including the belief we may have held in our twenties that we were going to live forever. And many of us, myself included, have experienced one (or more) health events that will impact our futures. That's why whenever possible, when it's in my client's best interest, I recommend a life insurance program that includes an appropriate amount of permanent life insurance as a foundation. For my married readers, I again point to the fact that about 70 percent of married women will be widowed. In many cases, for these women life insurance is the difference between a secure financial future and struggling financially.

Taking Care of *Your* Business

They burned down the gambling house; it died with an awful sound.
—*"Smoke on the Water," Deep Purple (1972)*

In late December 1971, the band Deep Purple was in Montreux, Switzerland, to record an album when the building where they were planning to record, the Montreux Casino, caught fire and burned to the ground. The band members watched the flames engulf the massive complex from their hotel, the dense smoke drifting heavily out over nearby Lake Geneva. Days later, bass guitarist Roger Glover woke from a dream of the fire with the title of a song rumbling around in his head: "Smoke on the Water."

The song, of course, tells the story of the "gambling house" fire and how "some stupid with a flare gun burned the place to the ground," shooting at the casino's dry rattan ceiling during a Frank Zappa and the Mothers of Invention concert. "Smoke on the Water" is now a timeless classic-rock hit, but it also serves as a cautionary tale to business owners about the many unexpected risks businesses face every day, including the unexpected death of an owner.

Because of this, small business owners in particular should know how important life insurance could be should the unexpected occur. In fact, every small business owner should be able to answer the following questions:

- Who unlocks the door if you can't?
- Who sits in your chair if you can't?
- Who talks to your customers if you can't?
- Who pays the bills and signs the paychecks if you can't?
- If you can't, then who will . . . and where will the money come from?

More often than not, if a small business owner dies without having a succession plan funded with life insurance, there's a strong chance that the business will struggle or possibly fold because there's nobody to take his or her place and no funds for the family to draw on until they're able to get things in order or sell the business.

Many business owners include their business as part of their retirement plan, and in some cases, *it is* their retirement plan because they think they can sell it when they retire. While in theory that may be true, what happens if something happens before they retire, such as a disability or death? Suddenly the owner isn't there anymore and the business immediately loses value because the person everyone is used to working with is no longer there, and there's no successor to take over.

In almost no time, that million-dollar asset has dissipated and either lost value significantly or gone out of business entirely. Sadly, I've seen it happen many times.

A business-succession plan includes two essential components:

1. A legally binding written agreement
2. The money to fund the agreement *and* keep the business running

To get small business owners thinking about these important steps, I often ask the rhetorical question: "Which is better: an agreement but no money or money but no agreement?" The answer is always the same: "The money, of course!"

Ideally, every plan should include both. In most business-succession plans, life insurance is often the most practical and affordable method to provide the money.

Benefiting from a Newer Kind of Life Insurance

No matter how I struggle and strive, I'll never get out of this world alive.
—"I'll Never Get Out of This World Alive," Hank Williams (1952)

Good ol' Hank Williams may predate the classic rock era by a few years, but his tune "I'll Never Get Out of This World Alive" speaks volumes to the foibles of life, and as much as we struggle, the only way out is when we up and die.

For many people, the value of life insurance seems to be a moot point because they don't see it as something to help them through life struggles— many think it only pays out after you die. But did you know that with certain types of relatively newer policies, you don't have to pass away in order to benefit from it? You can, in fact, be the beneficiary of your own policy through a relatively newer kind of life insurance policy that includes "living benefit features." A living benefit feature allows the policy owner the option to access a portion of the policy's death benefits in the event that, for example, he or she becomes chronically ill and ends up in the nursing home (which, as I mentioned in chapter 3, is very costly). In other words, you use up some of the policy's death benefit for certain real-life events. You are your own policy's beneficiary. Other living benefits can include up to a

100 percent return of premium after a certain number of years and access to a portion of the death benefit for terminal illness.

Many insurance companies offer living benefit features at no additional premium.[6] And while Hank's words about not getting out of this world are true, with a little bit of planning and with the right products, it is possible to have some protection though the many struggles and strifes of life.

I am not suggesting that everyone who reads this book should consider buying additional life insurance. However, learning more about the newer breed of life insurance with living benefits might be a good idea for you and perhaps the younger members of your family too. As with any decision, financial or otherwise, I suggest that you get the facts, evaluate them, and then decide.

Quick Riffs:

- Life insurance allows you to live each day as if it were your last. One day it will be!
- It's bad enough to die . . . don't do it for free.
- Don't let your liabilities outlive you.
- There is absolutely no advantage in waiting to buy life insurance. You will be older, your health could change, and worst of all, you might die!
- The best time to buy life insurance was yesterday—but that's no longer an option.

---

6   Benefit features vary by state and may not be available in all states. Utilizing this feature will reduce the cash value and death benefit.

Playlist:

1. "That's Life," Frank Sinatra (1966)
2. "Life in the Fast Lane," The Eagles (1977)
3. "Life's Been Good to Me," Joe Walsh (1978)
4. "It's My Life (And I'll Do What I Want)," The Animals (1965)
5. "Stairway to Heaven," Led Zeppelin (1971)
6. "The September of My Years," Frank Sinatra (1965)
7. "Touch of Grey." Grateful Dead (1987)
8. "Young at Heart," Frank Sinatra (1965)
9. "I Don't Need No Doctor," Humble Pie (1971)
10. "I'll Never Get Out Of This World Alive," Hank Williams (1952)
11. "Far Away Eyes," The Rolling Stones (1978)
12. "(I Can't Get No) Satisfaction," The Rolling Stones (1965)
13. "Mony Mony," Tommy James and the Shondells (1968) (Inspired by a life insurance company: Mutual of New York!)

Watchlist:

1. *Double Indemnity* (1944)
2. *If a Body Meets a Body* (1945)
3. *The Postman Always Rings Twice* (1946)
4. *RoadBlock* (1951)
5. *The Wrong Man* (1956)
6. *It's a Wonderful Life* (1946)

LIFETIME INCOME CALCULATOR

People tend to insure the replaceable things they own (home, auto, business) up to their full value.

What Is the Replaceable Value of your:

HOME $_____   AUTOS $_____   BUSINESS $_____

What is the amount of replacement Insurance you have on your:

HOME $_____   AUTOS $_____   BUSINESS $_____

What about your life, which is irreplaceable? Have you ever thought about the fortune that you'll earn if you live and keep your health?

YOUR CURRENT AGE	YEARS EXPECTED TO WORK	ANNUAL INCOME $25,000	ANNUAL INCOME $50,000	ANNUAL INCOME $75,000	ANNUAL INCOME $100,000
25	40	$1,885,031	$3,770,063	$5,655,094	$7,540,126
30	35	$1,511,552	$3,023,104	$4,534,656	$6,046,208
35	30	$1,189,385	$2,378,771	$3,568,156	$4,757,542
40	25	$911,482	$1,822,963	$2,734,445	$3,645,926
45	20	$671,759	$1,343,519	2,015,278	$2,687,037
50	15	$464.937	$929,946	$1,394,919	$1,859,891
55	10	$286,597	$573,194	$859,791	$1,146,388
60	5	$132,728	$265,457	$398,185	$530,914

Note: Assumes a 3% annual adjustment and working years to age 65

Determine your Estimated Lifetime Income Potential. For example if you are age 40, you could work another 25 years. If your current income is $75,000 you could earn a fortune of over 2.7 million dollars before you retire.

YOUR ESTIMATED LIFETIME INCOME POTENTIAL $_____

FACE VALUE OF YOUR LIFE INSURANCE $_____

How does the percentage of replacement value of insurance you own on your replaceable assets compare to the percentage of life insurance you own on your lifetime income?

Are you Financially Prepared if You Die or Become Disabled?

CHAPTER 5:

Another Brick in the Wall: Other Types of Insurance

Take a straight and stronger course to the corner of your life.
—*"I've Seen All Good People," Yes (1971)*

Just as there's no one "type" of classic rock style—exemplified by the psychedelic sounds of Pink Floyd topping charts around the same time as the country-influenced hits of Lynyrd Skynyrd—there are also many different types of insurance apart from life. And each one can play a vital role in crafting and protecting your ideal financial plan, depending on your needs and your family's needs.

Think of it as building a financial pyramid. The first step would be to fill in the bricks at the bottom, and then build from the foundation to the top. Liability insurance, life insurance, disability insurance, and health insurance are on that fundamental floor. That way, as you add, if one or more of the bricks are pulled from the top, then there might be some damage, but your structure is still intact. If you remove one of those foundational bricks, though, you could have a catastrophe on your hands.

There are several factors to consider when deciding which insurance policies are best for helping you build the plan, but first, I want to give you a brief overview of the different types of insurances out there.

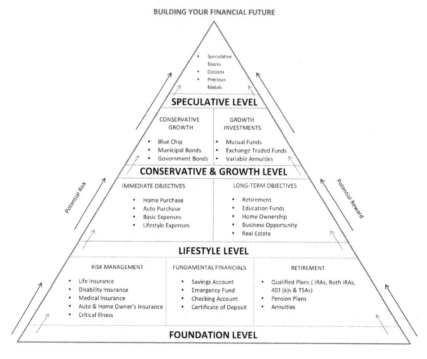

Build from the bottom up starting with a solid foundation.
As the potential reward increases so does the potential risk.

Disability Income/Paycheck Insurance

Take this job and shove it, I ain't workin' here no more.
—*"Take This Job and Shove It," Johnny Paycheck (1977)*

It's one thing to tell your boss to shove it and walk off the job. It's quite different when you're sick or hurt and unable to work. When the money needed for essentials such as food, clothing, and shelter is interrupted, there can be deep and immediate consequences.

Disability income protection insurance is for folks who are still working and earning regular income. Without it, if you get sick or injured and cannot work, the income stops. I recommend that you have at least 60 percent of your gross income insured, which is usually about what you net after taxes. That is particularly important in the last five or ten years of your employment because that is probably when you are making the most money, and you have the most to lose or forfeit if you become disabled. Having your income insured in case of a health event, an accident, or sickness is important and something that our firm believes is fundamental to having a proper plan. After addressing the risk of death or disability, you can comfortably begin to contribute to your long-term retirement plan.

You may already have a disability income insurance benefit from your employer. However, if you are self-employed and do not have insurance benefits, I encourage you to meet with your advisor and design a properly structured disability income/paycheck insurance plan. Without it, your income is at risk if an illness or injury prevents you from working before you are ready to stop. Once you are retired, you cannot purchase this type of insurance anymore.

Accidental Death Insurance

Suddenly I saw that we never ever would arrive. He put the plane down in the sea. The end of Flight number 505 . . . the end of Flight number 505.
—*"Flight 505," The Rolling Stones (1966)*

I am not certain of the origins of the tune "Flight 505" from the Stones 1966 album *Aftermath*, though it may be in reference to the flight that launched their debut US tour in 1964: BOAC flight 505.[7] Regardless of the

---

7   Neil Cossar, *This Day in Music: An Everyday Record of Music Facts* (Omnibus Press, 2014), p. 165.

song's genesis, the tune makes a somber point about the risk of accidental injury or death that follows us every day of our lives.

For people who live active lives or work physical jobs, accident-only insurance policies can be a lifesaver. I call it "just in case" insurance. This type of insurance can be especially beneficial for people who may not be able to qualify for life insurance due to health or occupation. Accidental death insurance is generally available on a guaranteed-issue basis and at an affordable cost, which is almost always worth it when you consider Jan and Dean's admonition that "You won't come back from Dead Man's Curve." Because no one expects to have to ask someone to "Tell Laura I Love Her," or to lose a "Teen Angel"—or even a "Leader of the Pack."

Casualty Insurance

He blew his mind out in a car. He didn't notice that the light had changed.
—*"A Day in the Life," The Beatles (1968)*

We know now that it wasn't Paul who blew his mind out in that famous Beatles tune, but whoever it was, in today's legal society, their estate would probably get sued.

Casualty insurance provides liability coverage for individuals and organizations for negligent acts or omissions. Say, for example, that you are involved in an auto accident and you are at fault. Subsequently, you have a lawsuit brought against you. If your auto insurance liability limit is $250,000 and you are found at fault for $500,000, I've got news for you. The other $250,000 is going to come from someplace, and that "someplace" is likely your assets because the court is not going to let you hide those.

If you have a million dollars of assets, the attorneys on the other side are probably going to sue you for more money because they are going to go after as much as they possibly can for this at-fault accident that you caused, no matter how sorry you are that you caused it. Even the people who are injured might say, "We forgive you." But they still want the money.

Simply put, it's an inexpensive way to have additional liability coverage that might not be covered under the liability limits on your auto or homeowner's insurance. This also comes in handy if you have a business and someone slips or another accident occurs on the premises.

When advisors do a financial analysis, they look at liability exposure, just to make sure that no hard-earned assets you set aside for retirement are put at risk.

Commercial Insurance

Commercial insurance is for business owners, and if the owner of the Montreux Casino so famously memorialized in "Smoke on the Water" didn't have it, I'm sure he wished that he did. For these types of clients, advisors work with commercial insurance firms who specialize in this specific type of risk. They come in and analyze the company and make sure they are properly covered, including evaluating where personal assets may be exposed, even if you think you may be covered.

Every business, large or small, should have this analysis done from time to time to see if there have been any changes in the law, different insurance codes from state to state, or any other unknown liability that the business owner might not be aware of.

Critical Illness Insurance

I don't need no doctor, 'cause I know what's ailing me.
—"I Don't Need No Doctor," Humble Pie (1971)

Maybe the members of Humble Pie didn't need a doctor (then again, maybe they did for lots of reasons we won't go into), but if you're stricken with a critical illness, you'll likely have many more expenses in addition to your doctor fees.

With critical illness insurance, the policy typically pays a flat amount upon proof of diagnosis of a defined critical illness. The two that most people think of first would be heart disease and cancer.

In my experience, when I was diagnosed with cancer, I became partially disabled. I was able to work, although I probably should not have, during the treatment period. My disability insurance company worked with me closely to do everything that could be done to pay a claim on my disability, but because disability insurance coordinates with income, I was still earning income in excess of what the contract called for. Because of this, I was not able to collect one penny of disability insurance, even though the insurance company approved my claim and would have paid had my income been lower.

On the other hand, if I'd had a critical illness policy, upon proof of my diagnosis I could have received a cash benefit, depending on the limits of my policy, of $50,000, $100,000, up to $250,000, even if I never missed a day of work. I would have had that cash to do with as I pleased, including pay off medical bills or just to put away or to make up for any income that I did lose.

Choosing not to purchase critical illness insurance when I could have was the biggest financial mistake I ever made. I was never sick a day in my life until age sixty-two—then *wham!* I had a very good disability insurance policy that would have paid me a lot of money if I was totally disabled, but I was not. Looking back, I would have benefited greatly from a critical illness policy.

You Can't Always Get What You Want

You can't always get what you want, but if you try sometimes,
you just might find, you get what you need.

—*"You Can't Always Get What You Want," The Rolling Stones (1969)*

Just like Mick Jagger didn't think he could actually get whatever it was he wanted, you may not be able to purchase policies for every type of insurance, and that is okay. You may be able to get what you need.

The best first step to getting what you need regarding the various forms of insurance is to meet with your advisor and have him or her analyze your situation, what risks and dangers you face, and then match those up to what you already have so you know what you are missing and where you may have potential risk. This will help you determine what insurance policies you need to purchase and what you can afford to do. You never know, you might actually get what you want, too.

You may, for example, find out that you have adequate life insurance and you do not need additional coverage. It's like getting a financial "physical," and just like any good doctor, an advisor is not going to recommend any treatment until he or she knows what you have going on.

If you and your advisor find risks in your current situation, the next step is to find out which pathway to take to alleviate that risk. Maybe you cannot buy more insurance because of a health event, in which case you need to have a plan B. Your advisor can put together recommendations based on your needs, your ability to pay, and other factors like your age and family status.

Even if you cannot afford everything you need, it is better to have something than nothing at all. A health insurance policy is not enough. If you have a great health insurance plan and you end up having a million-dollar claim, you are going to be glad you have that plan. The doctor, the hospital, the specialists—they all get paid. But what about you? What if you are no longer able to work? If you die, what is your family going to do? The health insurance policy will not help you then. It pays everybody but you. You need to make sure you have something that pays your family if you become disabled—something that helps keep your family afloat.

Once you have taken care of those essential needs and you have a plan together for when things fail and fall, you can take a deep breath and start planning for all the happy things you hope will happen in your future.

Quick Riffs:

How can different types of insurance help you build a more solid life plan? Before going to speak with your advisor, consider what needs you think you may have beyond the standard life and health insurance policies.

- Do you drive a lot for work?
- Would your current policy cover you if you were at fault in an accident?
- What about your company health insurance? Would it cover you if something catastrophic happened?
- Would your business be covered if something happened?
- How much are you covered in case of an accident?
- When was the last time you had your liability assessed?

Playlist:

1. "Flight 505," The Rolling Stones (1966)
2. "Dead Man's Curve," Jan & Dean (1964)
3. "Tell Laura I Love Her," Ray Peterson (1961)
4. "Teen Angel," Mark Dinning (1960)
5. "Moody River," Pat Boone (1961)
6. "Smoke on the Water," Deep Purple (1972)

7. "American Pie," Don McLean (1971)
8. "A Day in the Life," The Beatles (1968)
9. "Leader of the Pack," The Shangri-Las (1964)
10. "The Bricklayers Song," Noel Murphy (1978)
11. "Stranded in the Jungle," The Cadets (1956)
12. "Take This Job and Shove It," Johnny Paycheck (1977)

CHAPTER 6:

Hold on Tight: Managing the Wealth You Have Built

When I find myself in times of trouble, Mother Mary
comes to me, speaking works of wisdom, let it be.
—"Let it Be," The Beatles (1970)

Okay, so Paul McCartney was almost certainly not talking about his investment portfolio when he wrote "Let it Be," but the song does describe one of the great quandaries about how to handle the bulk of your invested assets as you go into retirement. Do you let them be, or should you structure things differently? Consider that when you're employed you have to work for your money. When you're retired, your money has to work for you. As I hope you learned from the previous chapter, there are differences between accumulation strategies and distribution strategies—and they are not subtle. If the great market meltdown of 2008–2009 taught us anything it's that care should be taken to plan accordingly.

Put simply, an investment is the process of spending something of value in the hopes that it will result in benefits to you down the road. You may have invested time in learning to play "Free Bird" on the guitar in the hopes of impressing a particular love interest or invested hard-earned dollars in a bus ticket so you could experience an epic music event like Woodstock. In the longer term, investing may allow you to one day afford all those things you dream about in retirement, and if you invest wisely, you may be able to do all of those things and more.

In many cases, appropriate preretirement planning relies in some form or another on investing in the stock and bond markets with the belief that over time your retirement account will grow and hopefully begin to blossom as you reach retirement. There are many ways to set money aside for retirement, but for now let's focus on some of the more popular methods such as your employer's 401(k) or similar plan or individually through an IRA. With the overwhelming attention the daily media gives the stock market, today's investors understand that markets don't always move up. They can and will go up, down, and sometimes sideways over long and short periods. Sometimes the ups and downs are slow and steady; other times they can be dramatic. Investors should be ready, willing, and able to accept this.

In a world that seems to get more complex on a daily basis, I strive to follow Albert Einstein's admonition: "Things should be kept as simple as possible but not one bit simpler." With that thought in mind, here's how I explain stock-market fluctuations. Imagine looking at the growth-pattern rings in a tree that's been felled. The years of healthy growth show up as wide and robust rings, meaning there was plenty of sunshine, nutrients, and water. Contrarily, the thin or even nonexistent rings indicate temperature changes, droughts, or insect damage. The tree still grew to a respectable height, even prospered, but what it took to get to that point was by no means steady or predictable. Markets generally work in similar fashion. The same goes with the financial accumulation stage of your life. But when all is said and done, the hope is that you've grown a tall, respectable, and mature "financial tree" that you can harvest from for a very long time.

This analogy is also a good way to explain why you shouldn't depend strictly on stock-market-correlated assets for your retirement income. Being tied to the stock market, there are times when those funds will rise and other times when they'll drop painfully low. The trick is to use those investments to create guaranteed income streams: the fruits of our labors.

Think about this. Suppose you were seeking employment and you received two job offers. You would want to know how you would be paid, right? One job paid you based on the movements of the stock market. For example, if the market goes up 10 percent, you get a raise. If it drops 10 percent, you get a pay cut. With this job there were no income guarantees. The other job paid you a reasonable salary commensurate with your experience and ability. Further, in profitable years, the company would pay you a profit-sharing bonus; however, in lean years, your base salary wouldn't be affected. Which job would you take?

When I ask people if they would consider the first job, most respond with something like: "That's crazy, I would never take a job like that! I want the one with the steady reliable income and the bonus possibility." Many of the retirees who consult me respond in similar fashion. Yet ironically, when I review how they have their retirement assets set up, they are doing precisely what they said they would never do, which is relying on their investment portfolio for retirement income and hoping for the best. This leads to the next question that begs asking: "If you wouldn't do that during your working years, why are you doing it in your retirement years?"

In retirement planning, it is my fundamental belief that stock-market-correlated investments be allowed to do what they were designed to do—potentially grow and prosper over the long term. Remember my tree ring example—that growth, although expected, can be sporadic. Liquidating stock-market-correlated assets needed for immediate income during periods of market decline can have dire consequences on your long-term retirement goals. Remember that accumulation is about the potential to grow your wealth. In retirement, the emphasis is on harvesting your wealth over what could be a very long period of time. This is, in a nutshell, why you should consider changing your attitude about accumulation and distribution once you retire. Hopefully you've accumulated money and invested in assets for the majority of your working years, and now you need to let those assets work for you by generating your retirement income stream.

The Stock Market Playlist

When considering investing in the stock market, it might be easier to look at it not as an intimidating mass of acronyms followed by glaring red and green arrows but rather as a gigantic playlist. There are hundreds of categories, from classic rock to classical, and within each are hundreds of subcategories with thousands of artists each.

For example, say you're looking for the Steve Miller Band to add to your playlist. You look under "classic rock," but that category has more artists under it than you can shake a stick at, so you further define it by looking under "blues & boogie rock," or if you're looking for Steve's earlier work, under "psychedelic blues rock." Eventually you find his albums and the songs that suit your listening needs.

The same goes for the stock market. There are the general categories such as "large-cap companies" with big company names (artists) under them like "Johnson & Johnson." These stocks are then broken down into stock types (songs) such as "value stocks" and "growth stocks."

Just as you would put your playlist together based on your listening objectives (your inspirational exercising playlist or your kickin'-back blues collection), you would go into the stock market with a specific objective and select stocks (songs) based on what you expect to get out of them. And like a playlist, unless you know exactly what you want to have on it, it's usually best to have an expert help you put it together. They might suggest stocks (songs) that you never would have considered or new ones that you fall in love with instantly.

On top of that, a good advisor will also help you coordinate your investments along with other income streams such as Social Security to help you organize all of your assets so that they provide you with the greatest possibility of success: the ultimate playlist to help you rock out your retirement!

It Doesn't Pay to Gamble

> *If you're gonna play the game, boy, you gotta learn to play it*
> *right. You've got to know when to hold 'em, know when to fold*
> *'em, know when to walk away, and know when to run.*
> —*"The Gambler," Kenny Rogers (1978)*

With that kind of advice, Kenny Rogers might have made a pretty good financial advisor. Because when it comes to selecting appropriate investments or putting together your investment playlist—also known as your portfolio—I caution against relying too heavily on historical performance. It's not predicable. It's like when a sports team pays millions of dollars for a player with hall-of-fame numbers only to find out he's past his prime; it can be a mistake to rely solely on an investment's *past performance* for your *future objectives.*

Sequence of Return Risk (a.k.a. Luck of the Draw)

Say we both own the same investment over a twenty-year period and that over the period its average annual return is hypothetically 8 percent. But say that you started to take withdrawals in the first five years, which happened to be the worst five years of that investment. I also take withdrawals over five years, but I do it later, which happens to be the best five years of that investment. After twenty years, your investment bucket may be close to empty because you started taking withdrawals on the downside, while my bucket may be close to full, even though the investment itself averaged 8 percent over the same twenty years. The luck of the draw, literally, went to me. The sequence of returns went against you because the market went down over the first five years of your cycle while the market was going up over the first five years of my distribution cycle.

That's the fallacy of using past performance because it can't be predicted. You don't know what tomorrow will bring, and that's how retirees can get in trouble— when they put all their chips on the table and use stock-correlated investments (meant to grow tall) for their retirement income. There is no such thing as a "guaranteed investment," and those who think there is can very easily crash and burn.

There's a time to take risk and a time to take it off the table. You've got to know when to hold 'em and know when to fold 'em, and don't ever rely on people who claim they can predict the unpredictable. I recommend taking a cautionary approach to investing, particularly as you approach retirement or if you're already retired.

To All There Is a Season . . . Including Retirement

Remember back in the 1960s when folk rock was big? One of my favorite tunes from that era is Pete Seeger's "Turn! Turn! Turn!" He was inspired to write it after reading passages from the Old Testament.

According to Pete, he came up with the melody in about fifteen minutes, then added the slightly altered biblical words and recorded it. The rest is history. The Byrds covered Seeger's version, making it the group's second number-one hit. (A cover of Bob Dylan's "Mr. Tambourine Man" was their first.)

The tune lyrically speaks to the fact that *to everything there is a season*. I believe that life's lessons prove those words to be true. I further believe that when it comes to planning for a successful retirement, *there is a time to take risk and a time to take risk off the table.*

When people engage me as their advisor, after helping them estimate how much income they will need to retire, one of the first questions I ask is, "How much of that income do you want guaranteed?" The answer is usually, "Well, all of it," or "As much as we possibly can." One way to do this is to allocate a portion of your retirement assets to a certain type of annuity contract called a single premium immediate annuity (SPIA). SPIAs are issued by insurance companies and are designed for people with a guaranteed income objective for a certain number of years—or for the remainder of their life or joint-lives, in the case of couples. When you purchase a SPIA, you exchange your principal (the amount you put in it) for a series of guaranteed payments that can be adjusted upward on a yearly basis for inflation. SPIAs are not designed for an accumulation objective. They are designed for people who want a steady and reliable income that won't be affected by future economic downturn.

It's important to remember that there is no single product or strategy that works every time for everyone. Always determine the financial strength of the insurance company issuing the annuity. You want to be sure the company will still be around and financially sound during your payout period. We encourage you to seek personalized advice from qualified professionals regarding all personal-finance issues.

What people tell me they like most about their Social Security and pension (if they have one) is "the check comes every month!" Steady, guaranteed lifetime income that can be adjusted for inflation can equate to some level of comfort knowing that you won't outlive it.

If it is true that *to everything there is a season,* retirement might be the season to take steps to reduce the risk to your income so you can enjoy a long, happy, rockin' and rollin' retirement.

Quick Riffs:

- For your long-term objectives, investing in the stock market is often more appropriate during the wealth-building or accumulation phase of life. However, it is not necessarily the best way to accommodate your retirement-income needs during life's distribution phase. An experienced advisor can help you select appropriate investments that are in line with the amount of risk you are comfortable with—your "risk-tolerance"—and your objectives.

- The only way to "time the market" is to know precisely when to buy and when to sell, and that is impossible.
- As you approach retirement, it pays to take a cautionary approach to investing.
- Diversification is a recommended way to reduce investment risk.
- If you are at or near retirement, to paraphrase the Four Seasons' classic hit "Let's Hang On":

Let's hang on to what we've got.
Don't let go we've got a lot.
Got a lot of "wealth" between us.
HANG ON, HANG ON, HANG ON,
TO WHAT WE'VE GOT.

Playlist:

1. "Let's Hang On," The Four Seasons (1965)
2. "Hang on Sloopy," The McCoys (1965)
3. "Hold On, I'm Comin'," Sam and Dave (1966)
4. "Hold On (to What You've Got)," Joe Tex (1965)
5. "Tighter, Tighter," Alive N Kickin' (1970)
6. "I Got You Babe," Sonny and Cher (1965)
7. "Turn! Turn! Turn!" The Byrds (1965)
8. "Let it Be," The Beatles (1970)
9. "The Gambler," Kenny Rogers (1978)

CHAPTER 7:

Seasons in the Sun: Life's Emotions, Relationships, Changes, and Detours

We had joy, we had fun, we had seasons in the sun, but the
wine and the song, like the seasons, have all gone.
—*"Seasons in the Sun," Terry Jacks (1973)*

This well-known tune by Terry Jacks is about a dying man lamenting the changes in his life. Jacks' version hit number one in the US, and in his home country of Canada, it was the top-selling single of all time up to that point.

Apart from death and taxes, change is another of life's certainties. There are the changes that come from choices before and after you retire—such as marriage, buying a house, and furthering your education—and there are the changes that come from unexpected detours—such as divorce, disabilities, natural disasters, and of course, death.

Changes happen all the time, but most of us don't think of life like that. We just assume everything will be hunky-dory . . . until it isn't. At that point, we can be lost at sea without so much as a life vest to cling to. It's not a fun thing to think about, but it's a necessary thing to plan for.

Warning . . . Warning . . . Danger . . . Danger!

If you have a fondness for classic 1960s TV, you'll know Robot's often-uttered line from *Lost in Space.* In virtually every episode, the nefarious Dr. Zachary Smith (no relation) fails to heed Robot's warning. Usually the space monster shows up, panels on the Jupiter 2 start exploding, and mayhem prevails. Call me "Robot" if you want to, but please heed my warning of possible retirement dangers. The best suggestion I have to prevent your retirement from exploding into mayhem is to sit down with an experienced advisor and take a look at the possibilities that lie ahead as well as the dangers and plan accordingly. Don't be like Dr. Smith and think you can avoid danger by assuming it's not there!

The foundation of any type of financial planning, whether business or personal, is adequate cash flow. For example, in a business, consistent *positive* cash flow is needed for profitability and growth whereas consistent *negative* cash flow usually leads to a business going under. That's why, when I prepare a financial plan for clients, I first determine their estimated expenses over the projected years of retirement, which could be twenty-five years or longer. I always factor in for inflation. Then I determine income sources such as Social Security (or similar) and pension (if there is one). This is called a cash-flow analysis. If income consistently outpaces expenses over the course of the plan, you will do just fine in retirement. When income sources are insufficient to meet expenses, you will have to begin drawing from your assets to make up the difference. Most people have to take the second choice—withdraw from assets. Therein is one of the greatest retirement dangers: drawing down assets at a faster pace than they can grow. Remember that if you live long enough (and I hope you do), inflation could overwhelm your income sources and you will have to take more and more from your assets. And turbulence in the market can significantly impact invested assets, so pay particular attention to what I said earlier about sequence of return risk in chapter 6.

If your investments won't last long enough, then you're going to have to start scratching out items on your budget that you're just not going to be able to keep once you retire, which is a sacrifice. So to minimize the need for sacrifices, it's important to plan in advance and not retire until you have a plan in place so that you can, hypothetically, see what the future looks like.

That hypothetical future is what we call your *financial roadmap*, and as we're creating it, we're going to look at it in relation to two important periods in your life: the happy time and the sad time. The happy time is when you and your spouse are in good health and you both have a sufficient income. You don't have to worry about whether the market is up or down because you've identified your base income and needs. You're able to travel and do the things that you imagined you'd do in retirement.

But then there's the sad time, which could be a health event or some other calamity, or an unexpected death where one partner dies far sooner than anyone expected.

To help baby-boomer clients plan for unexpected misfortunes, our firm uses software that illustrates examples of what would happen to your finances if the worst thing you can imagine happens—an unexpected death. It shows you how that would affect your Social Security and how it would impact your finances days, weeks, months, or years down the road. Again, it's not a fun thing to consider, but it helps our clients understand the "what-will-happens" when the "what-ifs" occur, and it helps them plan accordingly.

The Emotion Behind Retiring

What a drag it is getting old.

—*"Mother's Little Helper," The Rolling Stones (1966)*

Mick and Keith's prophetic words about the "emotional" side of aging was one of the first, if not *the* first, classic rock tune about pill popping and its consequences. "If you take more of those you will get an overdose," Mick and Keith sing, adding that "life's just much too hard these days."

So far this book has been about the financial aspect of retirement, but something you should also keep in mind as you approach the retirement threshold is the emotional aspect of it. There are challenges in adjusting to retirement, particularly in marriages, and the additional time spent together can be constructive, or in some unfortunate cases, destructive.

Several years ago I knew a couple who owned a very robust travel agency that they partnered in, and as they started to approach their retirement years, they decided to sell it. The travel business can be pretty hectic and high pressure, so I remember the wife particularly looking forward to the day when they could turn the key over to their successors.

When that day came, however, the husband had a very, very rough time adjusting to retirement. It got to the point where they would come into my office and argue until she started crying, and they would both walk out. Then she would come back in on her own and say, "Danny, I don't know what to do with him. He's just not used to having all this time on his hands."

They were both prepared for retirement financially but hadn't even thought about the emotional side of retirement. It's an intangible, and just as there are counselors out there that deal with post-traumatic stress disorder and emotional issues, there are counselors that specialize in helping people through the psychological distress of retirement. That kind of service is out of the range of a financial advisor, but we certainly know how to find people who can help clients with that if it becomes an issue.

And the problem isn't always that a spouse is married to his or her job, either.

I had another couple come to me recently regarding the emotional difficulties surrounding retirement. In this case, the wife did not want the husband to retire because she was convinced—as I was—that he was retiring too soon and they weren't financially stable enough to afford it. But his mind was made up. One day he said to me, "Danny, I've got to get out, I'm tired of what I'm doing." He said this even though he saw the same numbers that his wife and I saw.

It happens all the time; people are so focused on getting to retirement that when I ask them if they know what their world is going to look like financially the day after they retire, or one year, five years, or even ten years after, they say, "We haven't even thought about that, Danny."

Don't you think you should? You're going to live a long time, and things are going to happen over that time period that might upset the apple cart. Why not sit down and take a look at what might happen during your happy time and what might happen during your sad time and work out some plans for these events.

Love and Marriage—for Everyone

Love and marriage, love and marriage, go together like a horse and carriage. Let me tell you brother, you can't have one without the other.
—*"Love and Marriage," Frank Sinatra (1956)*

It may not be the first thing you think about after tying the knot, but at some point—hopefully sooner rather than later—you need to ask your partner, "What is our world going to look like the day after we're both retired?"

If you've already asked this question of each other, God bless you, but if not, then this question can be an attention-getter. Most couples are so focused on their day-to-day lives that they don't consider how they're actually going to achieve a happy and successful retirement.

The truth is, creating that ideal retirement plan isn't something that happens overnight. It's a long journey that may be fraught with many perils. I hope it's not, but risk is always involved in any of life's undertakings. If you went to the airport, for example, and had to choose between taking off in an airplane with a pilot and one without a pilot, which one would you choose? The one with the pilot, obviously, and the same should go for your retirement planning.

Relationships: I Love You Just The Way You Are

In 1977 Billy Joel sang, "I love you just the way you are," and that's truly the case for any relationship. Years ago, I began expanding my practice to help same-sex couples plan for their futures. I called my friend and colleague, Lindsey Smith, (no relation) who is a partner at a very prestigious Cleveland law firm. I wanted to make sure that his firm had the right experience to help.

"Let's talk face to face," I told him. "I have an important question to ask you."

So we met at my office, and he said, "Okay, what's the question?"

"I am working with a same-sex couple that requires some legal work. I want to know if your firm has experience in that area, and frankly, your personal thoughts before I recommend you," I said.

Lindsey couldn't have been more open.

"We work with all types of couples." he said.

"There's no reason we shouldn't get together and meet your clients."

Lindsey and I both agree that all people are entitled to the same representation. The partnership has worked out well for many couples, and we continue to work with that firm to this day.

Every now and then someone will inquire: "Danny what kind of people do you work with?" With a chuckle in my voice I respond: "Well, all kinds!" I've been doing this for a long time—more than thirty-five years. I've done work for nearly every ethnic group except Eskimos. I've worked with people who, in our current lexicon, would be labeled as straight, gay, transgender—you name it. I don't have a special process for one group or another.

Why is this? Well, if there's one thing that experience has taught me it's that people, regardless of ethnicity, lifestyle, or background, want pretty much the same things out of life. The simple answer is that, at least in my experience, same-sex couples want the same thing that everyone else wants. They want to have a sufficient income. They want to live in a safe neighborhood, drive a nice car, have money in the bank, and have a steady income. And yes, like almost everyone else, they want to retire someday.

Over the years, I can't recall any same-sex couples—or for that matter, individuals of what might be considered alternative lifestyles—asking me to plan any differently. The laws have actually been strengthened to recognize same-sex couples, particularly since the Supreme Court's ruling in *Obergefell vs. Hodges* that same-sex couples have the fundamental right to marry, so protecting their assets and helping them with their overall financial planning is not as much of a challenge as it used to be.

If you're in a same-sex relationship or another type of relationship the media would call an "alternative lifestyle" and want to start planning for your future, it's not a bad idea to call an advisor before you come in and say, "Do you work with, and have you worked with, same-sex or alternative lifestyle couples?" Personally, I like to take the opportunity during the Discovery Session, before any planning takes place, to say, "Before

I interview you, why don't you interview me? Ask me any question you want." I want everyone I meet, regardless of ethnicity, gender, sexual orientation, or age, to be comfortable with the way my staff and I conduct ourselves and to be confident in knowing that, first and foremost, we're here to help. I am extremely proud of the diversity in my own family and among the people I call my friends.

Love is an intangible emotion that is much easier to describe than it is to define. Classic rock is loaded with tunes about love and falling in (and out) of love. *But exactly how do you fall in love?* There's no rule book or set of directions that I know of. You just know it when it happens. Moreover, love comes in all shapes and sizes among people of all lifestyles. For example, the love we have for our parents, spouses or partners, and children is different than the love we have for our favorite sports team or classic rock band. The point is that love in any type of personal relationship brings with it the responsibility to have a plan in place—*to do the right thing if you will*—just in case something happens that could shatter our plans for the future.

D-I-V-O-R-C-E

Set me free, why don't you, babe? Get out of my life, why don't you,
babe? You really don't want me, you just keep me hanging on.
—*"You Keep Me Hanging On," The Supremes (1967)*

Regardless of when it happens, getting back on track financially is difficult after a divorce, and financially, you're never quite the same afterward. You may be getting part of your ex-spouse's wealth in terms of your retirement plan, but you're losing half of it, too.

Divorce, unfortunately, is not always an expected event. For younger couples, one spouse might come down with the "seven-year itch" (which in the movie provided the defining moment in Marilyn Monroe's all-too-short career—remember the breeze coming up though the sidewalk grate and blowing her dress in the air?). There are postretirement divorces when couples realize that they got along better when they weren't together a lot and others where it just seems to come out of the blue. Sometimes, to quote the Jerry Lee Lewis tune, one spouse gets the mental disorder called "middle-age crazy" even though by retirement they're well beyond middle age!

I talked with some clients recently who spend half of their year in a retirement community in Florida, and the wife was telling me about all of the issues they have with infidelity in this little homogenous community and the divorces that result from it.

Another couple that I recently worked with couldn't wait for their divorce to be finalized and, unfortunately, there was a high degree of animosity. "I hate that S.O.B." is not a practical divorce-planning tool.

The biggest issue, to me, was that they hadn't really thought beyond the divorce. They were so focused on the emotional baggage of getting to and then through the divorce that they hadn't thought about what their worlds were going to look like financially the day after, even though it would be easier and healthier to talk about it beforehand. Because once all was said and done and they were free from the liability of their ex-spouse, they suddenly found out about all of the liabilities that divorce can bring from the financial side.

Whether you see it coming or not, the most important thing you can do postdivorce is to just have someone to talk with—someone you trust who you can talk things over with and who can give you a bird's eye view as to where you are financially now that your divorce is concluded.

A predivorce financial review can be vital. Attorneys are often just trying to get the divorce over with as quickly as possible because that's typically what the client wants. But it helps to have a second set of eyes to help ensure that everything is equitable for both sides. There are pensions, for example, or Social Security, which any divorced spouse has a right to if they've been married more than ten years. And what about those life insurance policies? Should your soon-to-be ex-spouse be required to keep them in force with you as the beneficiary? A good attorney can help you sort all this out, and a good advisor can also recommend ways that can help you come out of the divorce with as much financial strength as possible.

Overall, if divorce lands on your doorstep, my firm can help. We help you reinvigorate and stay on the right track financially. But the quicker you start planning your future postdivorce, the quicker you can get back on track, even though it might not be the track to which you'd been accustomed.

Second Marriages

Who can say what brought us to this miracle we've found?
There are those who'll bet love comes but once, and yet
I'm oh, so glad we met the second time around.
—*"The Second Time Around," Bing Crosby, from the movie* High Time *(1960)*

Fifty/Sixty-seven/Seventy-four.

No, it's not a hit tune by *Chicago*. What these numbers represent— and this might shock you—are the percentages of first, second, and third marriages that end in divorce.[8]

In my experience, when someone gets a divorce for the first time, there's a high probability that they're going to get remarried. But the risk of another divorce is much greater that second time around.

For baby boomers, there are almost always questions about the new family structure. In all likelihood there are children on both sides from first marriages, and each new spouse has assets that they're not sure how

---

8   Jay Granat, "What to Watch for Today," http://www.divorce360. com/divorce-articles/after-divorce/love/why-do-second-marriages-fail. aspx?artid=1686

to allocate without offending anyone. A trusted advisor can sit down and discuss that and see what can be done to make sure that both sides can hopefully get along with their new family members.

One question that the kids may bring up is who's going to get the money when mom and dad remarry. This question can cause a lot of consternation and a lot of emotional baggage. But kids aren't the only ones who go into second marriages and hit a painful emotional wall. I've had newly remarried spouses come to me crying and saying, "I don't know why my husband's kids treat me the way they do," or "I don't know why my wife's kids reacted the way they did to this marriage. I want to be friends with them, and I love her. Why are they treating me this way?"

I wish I had answers to these types of complex issues. More than anything I wish that I could always come up with solutions that bring peace and harmony to everyone involved. In my experience, sometimes things get worked out and frankly sometimes they don't. If you're in a situation like this, the best advice I can give is, in order to get things worked out, first they have to be worked on. I suggest that you sit down with an experienced financial advisor who, in collaboration with an estate attorney if necessary, can map things out and then financially structure things in a way that might (at least) come close to keeping everyone happy. Remember that this is not so much a legal thing as it is an emotional one—and emotions usually trump everything else. Talking with someone with experience is a good first step. I know it's not easy. We are here to help!

Death and Dying

This is a happy story about death. You might wonder how it can be a happy story, but it is.

Last year, I lost a client who started investing with me when she was in her eighties. She had all adult kids and one day, several years after we started working together, I said to her, "Mrs. Jefferies, don't you think you should bring your kids in?"

"Why do I need to bring my kids in?" she asked me. "I've been alive for over eighty years. I know what I'm doing."

She liked owning mutual funds, and my concern was that she might pass away when the market was south of where she started. But she lived until she was just three weeks shy of her 102nd birthday. Before she moved into assisted living, she lived in the same little house where she'd raised her family and continued to live even after her husband passed away in the 1980s. She had one bad day in her life health-wise, and that was the day she died.

She was fine the day before and passed peacefully with no suffering. She had a lot of great days in her 102 years, with a few bumps in the road like we all do, and on the day she died, it was peaceful and her family was with her.

When I went to the funeral, it was not a sad occasion. Every one of her five adult children were happy to have had their mother with them for so many years. When they lost her, it was peaceful, and it was the way she wanted to go.

How could there be a happier story about death? It's not all about being remorseful and the bad things that can happen.

For her children, the other happy part of that story was that she was able to leave them some money. Even though I encouraged her to spend it, she would always reply that she was "leaving it for the kids." I recall that on a couple of occasions I would run into one of her sons. He always said that neither he nor his siblings wanted their mom's money. All I could tell him was that her mind was made up.

"I think she's worried that you're all broke," I would tell them, even though I knew none of them were.

But that is what she said she wanted, just as a lot of moms want for their children. My own mother struggled and strove to leave behind what little she did for my brothers and me. She wanted it for us even though we didn't need it. It was her wish, and we accepted that.

How to Move Forward Going down the Road . . .

Sometimes we're so focused on getting to a certain point, such as through a divorce or to retirement, that we lose sight of what happens the day after. Not only is it important to talk about this, but there's an incredible value in being able to talk about these kinds of things face-to-face with someone who can provide you with more than just an information dump; he or she can provide you with knowledge.

This is something that's lost in our day and age when you can go online and get doused with buckets of information but not that specific knowledge that comes from speaking to an expert one-on-one who looks at your specific situation and gives you specific, personal advice.

Here's a short personal story. To paraphrase the Grateful Dead, I was going down the road feeling bad . . . real bad! It's about the day after I'd been hospitalized for a week with severe nausea and dehydration from the side effects that come with chemotherapy and radiation treatment to the neck area for the type of cancer I had—squamous cell carcinoma. My throat was practically swollen shut, and the pain to swallow was so intense that even the liquid morphine I was prescribed didn't help. I was down to 135 pounds, receiving all of my nourishment via a feeding tube and feeling just terrible. I went to my oncologist and basically told him that I wasn't sure if I could keep up the treatment.

"This is nuts," I said. "It's not the disease that's affecting me, it's the treatment."

"Danny," he said, "there are two types of people I treat who have cancer. There's the kind like you who are going to get better, and there are the ones who aren't. When the ones who *aren't* going to get better tell me that they want to stop treatment, I don't try to talk them out of it. Because the treatment may add a few months or a year to their lives, but it may be the worst months of their lives. They might enjoy life more without the treatments.

"But in your case, Danny, you're going to get better. I'm not going to let you stop the treatment. Because you're one of the lucky ones—and if you finish this, you're going to get better," he said.

How could I possibly look at him and say I wasn't going to go forward with the treatment? He was telling me, in so many words, to man up, and I needed that on that day in my life. I went forward with the treatment, and I'm glad I did.

The knowledge and strength you gain from an interpersonal relationship with someone who's experienced in a specialized field is immeasurable. If I'd read the very same words that my doctor said to me on a website instead of hearing them from him face-to-face, I might not have gone forward with the treatment. Anyone who has undergone radiation treatment to the neck area will tell you that the side effects can be debilitating. But thanks to my doctors and the wonderful people at the Mercy Cancer Center in Elyria, Ohio, and the Cleveland Clinic, the biggest side effect is also the best one—full recovery! For all of my readers who are also cancer survivors, please reach out and share your story with me.

Speak with an expert, garner knowledge, and address the dark and ugly things that no one else *wants* to talk about but you know that you *need* to talk about if you're going to make it through those times without irreparable damage to your life and finances. And then move forward to the happy times.

Quick Riffs:

- Whether you're getting married for the first time or the seventh, having a retirement plan in place as soon as possible can make a difference in whether or not your retirement is successful.

- Many more financial protections exist for same-sex couples today, but it's a good idea to ask your advisor if he or she has worked with same-sex couples before to ensure awareness of the various laws involved.

- In the unfortunate event of a divorce, having a financial advisor review the assets for both sides can help ensure an equitable division of all assets involved.

- Even though we don't want to think about it, planning for health events and the great eventual—death—can make these difficult events much easier to handle.

- The value of an interpersonal relationship with an expert is immeasurable and can mean the difference between an effective financial plan and one that fails because it depended solely on information, not knowledge.

Playlist:

1. "Seasons in the Sun," Terry Jacks (1973)

Emotions

1. "Mother's Little Helper," The Rolling Stones (1966)
2. "I Second That Emotion," Smokey Robinson & The Miracles (1967)
3. "They're Coming to Take Me Away, HA-HAAA!" Jerry Samuels a.k.a. Napoleon XIV (1966)
4. "Emotional Rescue," The Rolling Stones (1980)

Love and Marriage

1. "Love and Marriage," Frank Sinatra (1956)
2. "Wedding Song (There is Love)," Peter, Paul, and Mary (1971)
3. "White Wedding," Billy Idol (1982)
4. "With This Ring," The Platters (1966)
5. "Still the One," Orleans (1976)
6. "When a Man Loves a Woman," Percy Sledge (1966)
7. "Everlasting Love," Carl Carlton (1974)

Relationships

1. "It Takes Two," Marvin Gaye, Kim Weston (1966)
2. "I Love You Just the Way You Are," Billy Joel (1977)
3. "Society's Child," Janis Ian (1966)
4. "What's Going On?" Marvin Gaye (1971)
5. "Lola," The Kinks (1976)

6. "Walk on the Wild Side," Lou Reed (1972)
7. "I'm a Man," The Spencer Davis Group (1967)
8. "I Am Woman," Helen Reddy (1971)
9. "Are You a Boy or Are You a Girl," The Barbarians (1965)
10. "Rock the Boat," The Hues Corporation (1976)
11. "Do Ya," The Move (1971) (Later as Electric Light Orchestra, 1974)
12. "Our House," Crosby, Stills, Nash & Young (1970)

Divorce

1. "D-I-V-O-R-C-E," Tammy Wynette (1968)
2. "Take Time to Know Her," Percy Sledge (1968)
3. "Memphis," Johnny Rivers (1964)
4. "Liar Liar," The Castaways (1965)
5. "She Got the Goldmine (I Got the Shaft)," Jerry Reed (1982)
6. "Jackson," Johnny Cash and June Carter (1967)
7. "Go Your Own Way," Fleetwood Mac (1976)
8. "Bread and Butter," The Newbeats (1964)
9. "You Keep Me Hanging On," The Supremes (1967)

Second Marriage

1. "The Second Time Around," Bing Crosby, from the movie *High Time* (1960)
2. "I'm Henery the Eighth, I Am," (also "I'm Henry the VIII, I Am"), Herman's Hermits (1965)
3. "Middle Age Crazy," Jerry Lee Lewis (1977)
4. "God Only Knows," The Beach Boys (1966)
5. "I've Passed This Way Before," Jimmy Ruffin (1966)
6. "Till There Was You," The Beatles (1963)

Death / Dying

1. "Honey," Bobby Goldsboro (1968)
2. "Last Kiss," J. Frank Wilson and the Cavaliers (1964)
3. "Patches," Dickey Lee (1962)
4. "Papa Was a Rolling Stone," The Temptations (1972)
5. "Endless Sleep," Jody Reynolds (1958)
6. "Dead Flowers," The Rolling Stones (1971)
7. "Hey Joe," Jimi Hendrix (1966)

Moving Forward

1. "Goin' Down the Road Feeling Bad," The Grateful Dead (1971)
2. "You Better Move On," Arthur Alexander (1961)
3. "Movin' On Up (Theme to *The Jeffersons*), Ja'net Dubois (1975)
4. "I'm Movin On," Elvis Presley (1969)

CHAPTER 8:

Gift Giving: Are You Hot-Blooded or a Cool Hand Luke?

*Saving up your money for a rainy day, Giving all your clothes
to charity. Last night the wife said, "Oh boy, when you're dead,
you don't take nothing with you but your soul. Think!"*

—*"The Ballad of John and Yoko," John Lennon (1969)*

How could John have known that just a few short years after he penned this song, he would be gone? "The Ballad of John and Yoko" is an eerily poignant tune that speaks to the challenges that the young and wildly famous couple faced on a daily basis, but it's also right on point about the fact that when you go, you don't take anything with you but your soul. What's the use of stockpiling wealth beyond your needs and the needs of your successors if it goes to no use?

The Grateful Dead was one group that absolutely understood the value of charitable giving and supporting charitable causes. For years, they did free performances for outreach groups and nonprofits before officially forming their charitable organization, the Rex Foundation, in 1983. Named for a former roadie-turned-road-manager, Rex Jackson, the foundation supports various causes that promote a healthy environment, the arts, social services, assisting the less fortunate, and protecting the culture and rights of indigenous people.

The Rex Foundation was the Grateful Dead's solution to an "overflowing cup" of wealth. Instead of continuing to accumulate wealth beyond what they could practically use, they chose to invest back in their community and put what they could toward bettering the world.

It's a great example of the two types of wealth that we build up in life: the physical and the spiritual. Spiritual wealth is made up of our beliefs, all those memories we accumulate, the life lessons, the nuggets of wisdom and, perhaps the greatest spiritual asset of all, love.

Physical wealth, of course, includes your tangibles such as money, property, and other assets in two asset types: replaceable and irreplaceable. *Replaceable assets* are just that: items that you could replace if you needed to—such as your home, your car, and your physical possessions. *Irreplaceable assets* are those less-tangible items, such as your health, your family, and your life.

Combined, physical and spiritual wealth equals your legacy—the gift that you hand down from the past to future generations. So gift giving, inasmuch as it can be physical, can also be the handing down of valuable memories, words of wisdom, or life lessons from grandparents to grandchildren and so on.

I like to help people with both.

Cold-Hand and Warm-Hand Giving

What we've got here is failure to communicate.
—*The Captain,* Cool Hand Luke *(1967)*

For years I struggled with a good way to explain the different types of charitable giving that people could engage in without making it sound like something that was only for the very rich. Then one day, after I'd been in the financial-planning business for about twenty years, I met a kind, retired accountant who explained to me the idea of cold-hand versus warm-hand giving. He'd read my firm's welcome kit, which included some information about our passion for helping clients leave something behind as well as give during their lifetime, and he remarked that he was glad to see it mentioned in our literature.

"You've been doing this a long time," he said. "Are you open to any ideas, young man?"

"Of course I am," I said, slightly flattered at being called young even though I was in my midforties at the time.

"For clients who show the desire to leave a legacy, ask them this question: Do they want to give with a warm hand or a cold hand, or would they rather do both?"

It immediately struck me as a far easier way to describe gift giving. There's the warm-handed giving you do while you're alive and the cold-handed giving that happens after you've passed on. It didn't have that only-the-wealthy connotation that tends to go along with words like "philanthropy" and "legacy," and I needed something that could convey that idea quickly and clearly. Because the fact is that almost everyone I come across in the United States has some degree of gift-giving desire, but they don't know how, or if, they can.

Our goal at Daniels Financial is to create at least $1 million in legacy gifts every year. These can be warm-handed, immediate gifts or they can be cold-handed gifts from people who have a little left after gifting to their children and grandchildren. If they don't have anything left when all is said and done, so be it, but in many cases there is, and we take care of that for them.

[Don't!] Keep Your Hands to Yourself

"Warm-hand" giving consists, of course, of gifts given during your lifetime, while "cold-hand" giving is done after you're gone. You can do either or both. If you have an "overflowing cup" and the desire to give, the first step is to set up a comfortable retirement mode so that you know you're never going to run out of money because your income is guaranteed. Then you have comfortable assets set aside so that you can make warm-handed gifts without worry. And then, if you have the desire, we can show you how to leave wealth to a prodigy or a charity after you're gone, a.k.a. cold-handed giving.

At my firm we have been very successful in helping people do this as well as doing it on our own. Every year we try to encourage our friends and clients to help us reach the aforementioned goal of $1 million, and we've been very successful at it. And it's very rewarding because people feel good when they make gifts, and certainly the receivers of the gifts feel good, and there are also people who know that they're going to go to their graves knowing that, after they're gone, their belief systems can continue through gifting—all because we sat down and showed them that they could afford to do it, if they wanted to.

For my wife and me, charitable giving is a way to repay the many blessings that we've had in our lives. It's good to know that when we're gone, the good things that we've helped to support will go on. So we make our gifts warm-handed, and we're going to leave some cold-handed money if there's any left. If there's none, then so be it. In addition to our local community foundation, we are also proud supporters of a nonprofit social movement dedicated to the betterment of humanity through promises made and kept called "***because I said I would***" founded by a remarkable young man named Alex Sheen.

Personally and as a company, building wealth on top of wealth does not motivate me. I'm more interested in helping people design retirement plans that give them the comfort of knowing that they're going to be financially secure throughout their retirement—that their income will never run out regardless of what the market does. Then if things work out, maybe they can set some money aside for family or friends or education or philanthropy during their lifetime and then again after they're gone.

My motto regarding wealth . . .

Employ it

Enjoy it

Pass it on

Eternal Rate of Return℠

Many of the people I work with share my belief in the importance of "leaving something behind" after they're gone. I have coined the term your Eternal Rate of Return℠. The more widely known term, after-tax rate of return (ATRR), measures what you actually make after such things as taxes, expenses, and fees are deducted from an investment.

I measure Eternal Rate of Return℠ by taking some gift-allocated assets and leveraging them—through life insurance, for example—so I can help clients create a legacy where money is passed on to charities, foundations, students, or loved ones who might need help in the future or, if done correctly, even in perpetuity. It allows my clients to know that they've done something good for humanity's sake, and the amount, large or small, doesn't matter. It's the thought that counts.

My wife and I are incredibly blessed to be able to support a "donor-advised fund" through our local community foundation that, once a year, selects area students to receive a gift that allows them to pursue their dreams through education. There are few things as gratifying as the handwritten notes we get every year from students thanking us for creating the fund and sharing how they're using the gift to pursue their dreams.

Another benefit of gift giving that I have the privilege to enjoy comes to me thanks to a former client, Mary Elizabeth Keller, who asked me to help her set up a fund for students at her alma mater, Kent State University. Although Mary passed away many years ago, Kent State still does me the honor of forwarding letters to me from students that Mary's fund helps to support. Her fund will go on for generations, and even though it wasn't my money that created the fund, it's gratifying to me to see her legacy living on. In Mary Elizabeth's case, you could call it her Eternal Rate of Return℠.

Legacy Planning: Memento Mori, Memento Vivere

Memento mori: Remember that you will die. This saying can be found on many ancient Roman tombstones because, for them, it was important to remember that life is finite. The full saying would translate to something along the lines of, "Remember that you will die, so leave as little to chance as possible." The reverse of that is *memento vivere*: "Remember to live." Combined, the sayings remind us to enjoy life today because tomorrow may never come.

In legacy planning, these phrases remind us to put our plans in place today because today may be all we have. This means not only planning your physical giving but also your spiritual legacy. Financial plans are more than just raw numbers. They can include recordings you made of memories that you'd like to pass on or albums with important pictures and memorabilia from your past. Memories, wisdom, and life lessons learned are just as valuable—maybe more so—as physical assets and should be treated as such.

I guess you could call me a late bloomer because, by the time I was born, all but one of my grandparents had died. The remaining one was my sweet, old Grandma Wise in my mom's hometown of Kent, Ohio. I can still remember going to her house as a boy and enjoying all those unique household aromas, like soup on the stove, as well as the nearby apple tree. I have those memories but little else, because when my grandma died, she took most of her memories with her. I'll never know what she was like as a child, what my grandfather was like, or what my mother was like as a little girl, because I was just too young to ask.

The loss of her and her memories is another reason I have such a passion for helping people with both the physical and spiritual aspects of legacy planning, and I remind them of memento mori but also memento vivere. Death is a certainty, but you also have a lot of living to do. Take care of what you can to smooth any potential bumps in the road, but don't forget to live your life to its fullest.

Life Insurance Legacies

The ability to leave a legacy can also be found in old life insurance policies. I meet many people who have policies for relatively nominal amounts— maybe $10,000 or $25,000—and they keep paying on them because they're victims of habit. Maybe they don't really need the life insurance anymore, because their kids are grown, the house is paid for, and they don't need the money in the policy.

In these cases, I'll ask if the policyholder has ever thought of simply changing the beneficiary on the life insurance to a church, school, or another charity that's close to his or her heart? It doesn't cost a nickel and you don't even have to tell the charity, if you don't want to: they'll find out after you're gone when the insurance company sends them a check in the mail. You can also choose to designate a portion of the policy's death benefit, say 10 percent to charity. You can do the same thing with annuity contracts, mutual funds or other assets that you own.

Another way that life insurance can be used by philanthropic-minded people is by purchasing a second-to-die policy. With this type of life insurance, two people—for example a husband and wife—are insured with the policy designed to pay the ultimate death claim when the last one dies (the survivor). These types of "survivorship policies" can be affordable because the insurance company spreads its risk over two lives instead of just one, and the policy owners can spread the yearly cost over many years.

When applicable, there is also a potential to reduce taxes with charitable-owned life insurance policies. Say, for example, that you're paying a $5,000 per year premium on a survivorship policy that is owned by a charity. Since you're the premium payer on the policy, but the owner of the policy is that charity, you may be able to receive a federal tax deduction for that $5,000 gift. If you're in the 30 percent tax bracket, then the government may give you a deduction of 30 percent of that $5,000, which means that $5,000 gift is only costing you $3,500 net.

For those with wealth that might be beyond what they will need in life, I'll often ask if they've thought of leaving a small percentage to a foundation, their church, or a favorite charity? This can be done with an amendment, a transfer-on-death form, or a change in beneficiary, allowing the bulk to go to family and that little bit to go to a worthy cause. An added bonus is that these actions don't require an attorney and a mess of legal documents.

If you want to do something a little more sophisticated, however, a qualified attorney partnering with your advisor can provide guidance on other ways to make either warm- or cold-handed gifts or a combination of the two. But if you just want to leave a little something behind to a good cause, partnering with your advisor, you can meet with a representative of your local community foundation and learn about how to create a donor-advised fund. Community foundations exist so "common people" often with big hearts but smaller wallets can leave something behind. I am a strong advocate of community foundations and the good work they do. Since state and federal governments regulate community foundations, the foundations take care of all the heavy lifting and only keep a small amount to help them cover expenses. It's one way to leave something behind through a warm- or cold-handed gift. And please remember that virtually all charities, churches, schools, universities, foundations, and other philanthropic organizations are happy to accept your generosity because "it's the size of your heart not the size of your gift that matters most!"

Planning for Education

There are a couple of ways to fund your children's or grandchildren's education through financial planning, one of which can be done through your life insurance policy. For younger parents especially, this can be set up at very little cost and will help ensure that their children's education is self-completing. In other words, if the unthinkable were to happen to you or your significant other, then part of your life insurance policy could be directed toward their education.

Another savings option is through a 529 plan or qualified tuition plan. What's great about this plan is that you don't have to own it to contribute to it, and when you do contribute to it, many states allow you to lower your state income taxes by whatever amount you put in. The rules do vary in each state, so before you invest, know whether you or your beneficiary's home state offers tax benefits for college savings plans.

These plans are also a great way to approach holiday gift giving. Instead of spending all kinds of money on gifts that the kids often barely use, parents can ask grandparents to only spend half of what they normally would on physical gifts for the kids and to put the other half in the 529 plan. I like to call these "split" Christmas or birthday gifts "now and later presents." The "now present" can be a toy and the "later present" a contribution to a 529 plan.

In fact, some 529 plan providers actually send holiday and birthday cards to the children to let them know that a loved one set money aside for their college education. It's a very practical gift with far-reaching benefits, and it lets the kids know that you love them and care about them and want them to have the best.

Even if the beneficiary decides not to go to college, the beneficiary can be changed to another person or to yourself if you've decided that you'd like to go back to college.

Opening a 529 plan is a great way to make a warm-handed gift that will last over the lifetime of your children, grandchildren, or any other kids you want to help. A good advisor can help.

A Wealth of Memories

There's a term I like to use when describing what we do as financial advisors: first and foremost, we help people create a wealth of memories. Because what's more important to you, a wealth of memories created when you're alive or memories of wealth after you're gone? Having a dynamic plan in place can help you to maximize your assets, determine additional sources of retirement income if possible, and use all of that to build a wealth of memories during your lifetime instead of being afraid that you might run out of money someday. So plan well, and if you have some extra fun-money, spoil the kids, spoil the grandkids, and if you so choose, contribute to a worthy cause. The greatest thing about a warm-handed gift is that you can get a hug and a thank you from someone whose life you've helped to make better.

Although donations to charities or churches are often tax deductible, in my experience, few people do it because of the tax deduction; that part is just icing on the cake. They do it because they want to make a difference, they want to give back to their community, and they want to say thank you for such a bountiful life.

Grandma's Ring: The Immeasurable Value of Writing It All Down

Another reason to consider warm-handed gifts is in the value of spending down and dividing your assets while you're still alive. If you talk with some families long enough, you may hear of a family unpleasantness "that happened when grandma died." By not writing down who gets what, even down to some of the most seemingly inconsequential things, you can unintentionally be the source of family divisiveness.

Take the old story of Grandma's ring. Grandma had a beautiful wedding ring that she wore every day since she married Grandpa so many years ago. The eldest of her four granddaughters was there with her when she passed away, and after Grandma's death, the eldest granddaughter decided to take the ring because, after all, Grandma had promised it to her, and she didn't want it to get caught up in the estate.

The problem, however, is that at different points, Grandma had promised that same ring to all three of her other granddaughters—and when they saw it on the eldest granddaughter's hand, they were furious.

Families have divided over these kinds of conflicts, my own included. When my grandmother passed, I remember going to her old house with my mom and aunt. While we were there, my two uncles showed up, and they all began arguing. I don't know what it was about—I was just a kid—

but it couldn't have been anything of real value, because my grandmother's estate was not that large. Whatever it was, though, it resulted in my mother and aunt not speaking to my uncles for almost twenty-five years.

Years later I got a call from my mom. My uncle Bob just had a heart attack, and she needed me to drive her and her sister, my aunt Helen, to see him. She wanted to mend the fence before it was too late.

As we walked into the hospital, my uncle looked up with tears in his eyes and could only say his sisters' names over and over. They hugged and cried, and all I could do was stand back and think, *My God, twenty-five years wasted over something as inconsequential as dining room furniture or whatever it was they were fighting over so long ago.*

It wasn't Grandma's fault, but by not putting her wishes in writing, it caused a huge rift in our family that lasted a quarter of a century. And there doesn't have to be a lot of assets in play to cause this kind of divide. Something as simple as a single wedding ring can have life-altering consequences.

Many people want to avoid this conversation—who gets what when they pass on—because they don't want to talk about their own death. But memento mori: we're all going to die. Sometimes I have to give people a gentle nudge as their advisor, but planning this type of distribution while you're alive eliminates a lot of strife after you're gone, and that's particularly true when there are second marriages.

One of the greatest gifts you can give is having a plan in place to let your family know how everything will be allocated. It solves a lot of problems and may even save whole families from unnecessary divides.

Quick Riffs:

- Wealth is both physical and spiritual. Leaving behind your memories and wisdom can be just as valuable, if not more valuable, than any physical assets you might leave behind.

- You can warm-hand give, which is giving to charitable causes while you're alive, or cold-hand give, which is donating assets after you've passed on. You can do either or both, and you don't have to have a lot of assets to make a big difference to a worthy organization.

- Creating a legacy is easier than many people expect. For example, old life insurance policies can be signed over to a charitable foundation or charity.

- Planning for your children's or grandchildren's education can be done through life insurance policies or by creating a 529 plan, both of which are very simple to set up and can have incredibly beneficial impacts down the road.

- When it comes to physical assets, help your family avoid any unnecessary conflict after you're gone and either warm-hand gift your assets now or write down your allocations so that no one can contest ownership.

- In gift giving, what matters most is the size of your heart, not your wallet or checkbook.

- Legacy giving allows you to "leave a little of your life" behind for others to harvest.

Playlist:

1. "This Diamond Ring," Gary Lewis and the Playboys (1965)
2. "With This Ring," The Platters (1966)
3. "We Are Family," Sister Sledge (1979)
4. "Turn Back the Hands of Time," Tyrone Davis (1970)
5. "Ring of Fire," Johnny Cash (1963)
6. "RINGO," Lorne Green (1964)
7. "The Ballad of John and Yoko," John Lennon (1969)

CHAPTER 9:

Taxes: Six for the Tax Man and One for the Band

If you drive a car, I'll tax the street. If you try to sit, I'll tax your seat. If you get too cold, I'll tax the heat. If you take a walk, I'll tax your feet.
—*"Taxman," The Beatles (1966)*

Question: When is a million dollars not a million dollars?

    a.)   If you win the lottery

    b.)   When it's in a pre-tax IRA, 401(k), or similar "qualified plan"

    c.)   When you win big at Monopoly

    d.)   All of the above

If you guessed "d," you are correct. Many people believe incorrectly that when the house and cars are paid for and all the bills are paid they are free from liability. But what about all that money you have in your pre-tax qualified plan? Suppose when you retire you end up in a 25 percent marginal tax-bracket. If I told you that the United States government, through its taxing authority the IRS had placed a 25 percent lien on your I.R.A. you might say, how can they do that? Well, they can do it because they can. It's what I call the good news—bad news lottery rule. If you win the lottery the good news is that you won. The bad news is that you don't receive a penny until the tax is paid. Money in pre-tax qualified plans is taxed in similar fashion. The good news is that you have (I hope) a nice balance in your retirement plan. The bad news is that, depending on your tax bracket, up to one-fourth or possibly one-third of it could end up as I.R.S. tax revenue instead of your retirement revenue. I'm not suggesting that there's a way around this. And yes, I believe in paying my fair share to live in our great nation. However, depending on your situation there may be methods to moderate the tax. I mean, why pay any more than you have to? My personal experience as an advisor is that people who fail to include a tax strategy as part of their financial plan often end up paying more than their fair share. That's why I take an active role to educate my clients on ways to minimize taxes. A qualified advisor working in tandem with your tax preparer can analyze your specific situation and possibly offer some ideas. By the way, the good news—bad news rule doesn't end when you die. The tax liability carries forward to your beneficiaries.

Most baby boomers remember the famous—or infamous—sports newscaster, Howard Cosell. One of the lines he was most known for was, "I'm going to tell it like it is." When I first sit down with new clients, I tell them that there are two types of people in my profession: those who tell you what you want to hear and those who take Cosell's approach and tell it like it is.

"Which one would you like me to be?" I ask them. "Do you want me to tell you what you want to hear, or do you want me to tell you what you *need* to hear?"

Every one of them says that they want me to tell it like it is. And I do because we all want to be told the truth, even though it may be hard to hear. Taxes are one of those areas where I often have to talk about things that people don't want to hear, but if they listen, they might come out the better for it.

Death and taxes are two of life's constants, but unlike our eventual eternal departure, sometimes taxes can often be modified or even reduced. The problem is that many people don't look at taxes that way. They go about life, send their paperwork to their CPA after the first of the year, and pay what they're told to pay.

But what if there was a better way? Instead of approaching taxes in a reactive manner, we could look at them proactively—and include tax management as part of your overall financial plan and potentially reducing your tax liability.

Is There a Better Way?

> *There must be some way out of here, said the joker to the thief.*
> *There's too much confusion, I can't get no relief. Businessmen,*
> *they drink my wine, plowmen dig my earth. None of them*
> *along the line know what any of it is worth.*
> —*"All Along the Watchtower," Bob Dylan (1967)*

Too much confusion? I think Dylan was singing about the US tax code!

If I asked you what you thought the tax environment would look like when you retire—if taxes would be higher, lower, or the same—what would you say?

Almost everyone would say, "They'll be higher."

If that's the case, I ask you, then why would you delay taking money out of a retirement plan? If taxes are only going to increase, which certainly seems to be the case if you take a look at debt-reporting vehicles such as the US Debt Clock (www.usdebtclock.org), then it might make more sense to look at what would happen if you started taking money out of your 401(k) or IRA earlier rather than later. For example, would you rather pay twenty cents on the dollar now and invest that money in other assets that can continue to grow, or pay thirty cents on the dollar when you withdraw it in five years if tax rates increase?

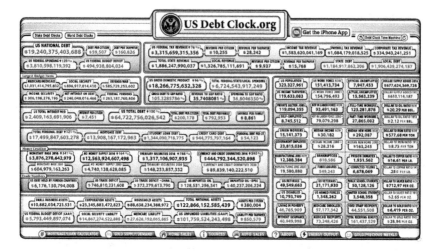

Waiting until a certain age to withdraw from your retirement account is simply sticking to a date that the government affixes to your money. You don't necessarily have to follow that—if you can make those funds work better for you in other ways by taking distributions from your retirement account now.

I'm not recommending that anyone start withdrawing from retirement accounts early, of course, but when you sit down with a financial advisor to plan your retirement, it only makes sense that they look at all of your assets and show you the most tax-efficient way to begin distributions.

I know that the conventional *rule of thumb* is to wait as long as you can to start withdrawing from your retirement plan (unless you need the money of course). But remember that the rule of thumb only works if the rule fits "your" thumb!

Taxes: Proactive vs. Reactive

Over the years I have worked with many people who have inadvertently overpaid their taxes. Because they didn't look for options to modify their taxes or didn't have a professional look for them, they simply reacted when it was time to pay taxes, added up what they owed, and sent it along.

Advisors, however, can help you approach your taxes proactively. As an advisor, I don't prepare my clients' taxes. What I try to do is work closely with their tax professional to see if we can team up and find ways to best manage taxes.

Experience has taught me that, in most cases, people overpay because they fail to fully coordinate their investment and income side of the ledger with tax obligation. Taxes, when not coordinated with your financial plan and other investments, can be the biggest drain on your retirement income every year—because regardless of your portfolio's status, you're more than likely going to pay taxes. On the other hand, including *tax efficiency* in the loop can be beneficial. I often ask people, "If working with me could reduce your taxes by a hundred dollars, would you do it?"

Many would reply, "Well, maybe. It's just a hundred dollars, so we'll have to think about it."

Then I ask, "If you were out walking on a windy day and a hundred-dollar bill blew out of your pocket, what would you do?"

Most people reply, "I'd chase after it!"

"Well, what if a stranger picked up that hundred dollars and made off with it, how would you feel?"

Just about everyone says they'd be angry, and some would even walk up and demand the money back.

Then I inquire, "Well why? It's just a hundred dollars."

When savings are theoretical, we often don't consider their value. But when we actually picture that loss in our minds, with a physical hundred-dollar bill escaping our pocket or with a stranger—otherwise known as Uncle Sam—grabbing it and keeping it, our priorities change. So why *wouldn't* you want to focus on things that you know will happen and make those a part of your priorities?

Coordinating Tax Liability with Tax Planning

You load sixteen tons and what do you get? Another day
older and deeper in debt. Saint Peter don't you call me
'cause I can't go; I owe my soul to the company store.
—*"Sixteen Tons," Tennessee Ernie Ford (1955)*

Tax planning and tax liability are almost always treated as two separate entities, even though they are not. Because regardless of whatever investment type you have, sooner or later that investment—if it makes any money—is going to generate some type of 1099 form.

A 1099 is essentially a form that an investment company, bank, or other entity sends to you and the IRS to report a distribution, be it from dividends, capital gains, retirement plans, or just about any other type of distribution.

Because certain distributions like income and dividends are taxed differently than capital gains, you could end up paying the maximum amount allowed by the IRS. How is this possible? Here's one example. Distributions from your IRA or 401(k) usually count as "provisional income," which shows up on your tax return. When your provisional income hits a certain level it causes up to 85 percent of your Social Security to be taxed and can substantially increase the amount you have to pay for Medicare Part B and Part D. That's why sometimes it makes sense to take smaller distributions from your IRA or 401(k) when you're younger rather than hold off until the mandatory age of seventy and a half, when it's really too late to do any tax-efficient planning on those distributions. I know this may seem counterintuitive to the conventional wisdom of waiting as long as you can to begin withdrawing from your retirement assets (unless of course you need the money), but in certain circumstance it can make sense to pay moderate taxes over a longer period of time than waiting to potentially pay much larger amounts. As part of our process we look at tax management as an essential component of your plan. We welcome the opportunity to team up with your tax preparer to see if, through a coordinated effort, we can minimize the heavy impact that taxes have on your future.

Many people fail to realize that one way to diminish your assets is by paying more taxes than you might have to. There will be years when investments go up or down, and even though there's the expectation that their value will go up over the long term, the ups and downs of the market are not predictable. Taxes, however, are predictable. You pay them every year unless your assets and your income sink so low that they become untaxable, and we don't really have a solution for that. So wouldn't you want to include in your financial plan a way to at least moderate or minimize your taxes?

Losing Your Best Tax Partners

I get by with a little help from my friends.
—*"With a Little Help From My Friends," The Beatles (1967)*

Another factor that is often overlooked in the tax-management process is what can happen to your taxes when the mortgage is paid off and the kids move out. Usually what happens is that your taxes increase sometimes dramatically. Why? Because two of your most reliable tax deductions— mortgage interest and your children—have disappeared from your tax return. I'm not saying that paying off the mortgage and having the kids move out is a bad thing. Sometimes it's a godsend. But for some people, for example those in higher tax brackets who are able to properly service their debt, it could be a good idea to consider maintaining a mortgage.

Home mortgages, when managed properly, can be an important component to your overall planning strategy because mortgage interest can be tax-deductible. As you pay down your mortgage, the interest you pay is reduced and along with it the amount that can be deducted. Fewer deductions mean higher taxes. Tax-deductible interest equates to lower taxes, which in a sense means Uncle Sam is rewarding you for living in your home. Mortgage interest is tax deductible. When you pay off a mortgage too soon, you lose what we like to call "good debt" or debt that's tax deductible. Before paying off a mortgage, it's a good idea to do a home-equity review to see if it might be feasible and beneficial for your taxes to carry some amount of good debt.

Many people don't realize that interest on a home equity loan (also called a home equity line of credit or HELOC) can be tax deductible. What's even more surprising is that if you finance that second home you have been dreaming about, interest on that mortgage can also be tax deductible. And that could include an RV as a second home. If you want to learn more about this topic, I suggest that you talk with your CPA or an advisor with knowledge in the area. With any type of tax planning, it's important to know the rules so you can follow them, and each person's situation is different. Always consult with your tax professional first to make sure if any of this applies to you.

Minimizing Your Taxes

Red and white, blue suede shoes, I'm Uncle Sam, how do you do? ... I'll
drink your health, share your wealth, run your life, steal your wife.
—*"U.S. Blues" Grateful Dead (1974)*

Apart from the possibility of using tax-deductible mortgage interest to your benefit, there are other areas where many people could save on taxes but don't often consider them.

Take Social Security. Many people believe that Social Security retirement payments are never subject to taxation when, in fact, up to 85 percent of your Social Security can count as income and be taxed. Whether you're on Social Security now or looking to take it in the future, have you looked at ways to minimize your Social Security taxation?

To do this, you will want to look at your income. Most types of income are taxed right away and count toward your tax liability on Social Security benefits. Deferred income, on the other hand, doesn't show up on your taxes. If you have a $100,000 accumulation annuity with a 4 percent return, for instance, then unless you take money out that year, you just made 4 percent or $4,000. By allowing money to accumulate inside a tax-deferred annuity, the income isn't taxed, and it doesn't count toward the taxes you have to pay on Social Security. So while you'll have to pay taxes on it whenever you do take it out, you can delay paying those taxes by putting money in places where it doesn't count as income today.

Medicare premiums are another area where savings are possible because Medicare Part B and D premiums are determined on a sliding scale upward, depending on income. This can surprise a lot of people because they may have talked with a retired friend about their Medicare costs, or their mom tells them what she's paying—but when they go into Medicare, they end up with a much higher premium because of their income. To make sure you head into retirement without any surprises, you should speak to an advisor *before* retiring about your Social Security and Medicare Parts B and D to get a clearer picture of your potential tax liability and ways you may be able to minimize it. Without a coordinated financial plan, your taxes could be the biggest drain every year on your retirement income.

You Can Pay Me Now . . . or You Can Pay Me Later

Years ago, back when people still changed their own oil, there was a commercial on TV for FRAM oil filters. The spot featured this big, burly-looking mechanic standing in a garage and talking about the benefit of changing your oil filter in a timely matter—and the detrimental effects of not doing so. At the end, the mechanic would say something along the lines of, "When you think about this, you can pay me now or you can pay me later." Then he would take out this dirty oil filter that clearly hadn't been changed in six years and throw it in the trash. Everybody got what he meant when he did this: you can pay a little now for a new filter—or possibly a lot later for a new engine because you weren't diligent in keeping your vehicle up to snuff.

It's something to keep in mind for your retirement planning as well as your car. Because that's just what Uncle Sam says: You can pay me now, or you can pay me later. And since Uncle Sam doesn't mind waiting, he might prefer it sometimes if you pay later, because he'll wind up with a lot more of your money—especially if taxes go up.

Permanent life insurance is another area where cash values can accumulate tax-deferred. When cash values in permanent life insurance contracts grow—as long as they're within contract and funded according to IRS code—then no taxes are taken out. In fact, if you *do* take money out of your permanent policy in later years, as long as you do not withdraw more than your basis (total premiums paid) and continue to properly fund the policy, that money still doesn't count as income.

Policy withdrawals are generally not subject to taxation up to the amount paid into the policy. Policy loans and/or withdrawals also reduce the cash surrender value and death value and increase the chance the policy will lapse. Taking a policy loan could also have adverse tax consequences if the policy terminates before the insured's death. Also, as we discussed in chapter 4, in most cases the death benefit from life insurance usually doesn't count as income and is paid tax-free when you pass away, as per Internal Revenue Code (IRC) 101. In essence, life insurance is one way you can build savings where the yearly increase in value does *not* generate a 1099 form and, consequently, taxes. Not only do you not have to report the increased value on your tax return, the increases left in the contract are not reported to the IRS.

Roth IRA plans are another way for you to save without having to be taxed for what you withdraw, as long as certain conditions are met. While you don't get a tax deduction for the money you put in, being able to withdraw funds down the road without having them considered to be provisional income could make a pretty big difference.

Where else can you go to have a conservative, long-term inclusion in your plan that offers these kinds of tax incentives? That's not to say that everyone should have permanent life insurance or a Roth IRA, but they are certainly options that people ought to be aware of.

In my experience, I've never met anyone who was upset that he or she didn't have to pay taxes on money taken out of a Roth IRA or from the cash accumulation inside a properly structured and funded life insurance contact. With emphasis on permanent life insurance, the internal build-up of cash within the contract (its cash-accumulation value) accumulates tax free—then it can be withdrawn tax-free under provisions in the contract, as per IRC 77(e) and IRC 7702.

Looking at Your Life after Retirement

I can't stress enough how important it is for people to think about their lives after retirement. If you don't look at what your taxes are going to be like, and if you don't form a plan early, then you may be in for a rude awakening. It takes more than just setting up some savings accounts to prepare yourself for retirement. Taxes are a constant, but they are a constant that can be manipulated, and if you aren't looking at all of your options, then you're doing yourself a disservice.

I suggest enlisting the help of an advisor who can help you determine if it makes sense to pay Uncle Sam now or wait to pay him later in the most tax-efficient way possible.

Home Equity Conversion Mortgage— What the Heck Is a HECM?

If I asked you if you knew what a "HECM" was you might say, "What the heck is a HECM?" But if I used the more common term of reverse mortgage you might respond, "Oh yeah, I've heard about them—but I'm not quite sure how they work."

Briefly, a reverse mortgage is a way for people age sixty-two and over to supplement their income with the equity they have in their home. A home equity conversion mortgage, "HECM" for short is a reverse mortgage insured by the US federal government. In financial jargon there are liquid assets and hard assets. A liquid asset is more easily converted into cash than a hard asset such as a home. A reverse mortgage is a way to "convert" a portion of your home's hard asset value into cash without having to actually sell it or make payments on a home equity type loan. I don't believe that every homeowner age sixty-two should consider doing a reverse mortgage. And I don't like some of the commercials I see and hear that make it sound that way. Although we don't do reverse mortgages at my firm, I do try and educate my clients about how they work if I'm asked to do so. A good resource for more information is the U.S. Department of Housing and Urban Development (HUD) website: hud.gov.

In conclusion, I remind you that even though some strategies may or may not be for you, it pays to educate yourself. For some people it makes sense to begin taxable distributions early, for others it makes sense to wait (defer). Step outside of your belief system regarding taxes for a moment and look at things from a different angle. You just might be able to work out some significant savings.

Quick Riffs:

- Stop being reactive and start being proactive about your taxes!
- Is there a better way for you to organize your income and assets so that it results in modified or even reduced taxes? Consider some of the following questions, and bring them to your advisor. The worst thing that could happen is that there's nothing you can do—but at least you know that you aren't missing out on any potential savings.
- Are you coordinating your tax planning along with your overall retirement plan?
- Are you withdrawing from your retirement plan at the most cost-effective time?
- Have you coordinated your distributions in such a way that you can delay, modify, or minimize your taxes?
- Would it make more sense to keep paying your mortgage instead of paying it off early, since it's the only interest that's tax deductible?

- Have you looked at your Social Security to see if you can minimize your Social Security taxation?
- Have you evaluated your Medicare Parts B and D to avoid sliding too high on the cost scale?
- Can any of your income be adjusted in order to move it from provisional to nonprovisional?
- Have you considered the advantages of a permanent life insurance policy in regard to using it as an account where cash value can grow tax-deferred?
- Would establishing a Roth IRA make sense for your retirement plan?

Playlist:

1. "Taxman," The Beatles (1966)
2. "Sunny Afternoon," The Kinks (1966)
3. "Fortunate Son," CCR (1969)
4. "Movin' Out (Anthony's Song)," Billy Joel (1977)
5. "Take the Money and Run," Steve Miller Band (1976)
6. "Help!" The Beatles (1965)
7. "I've Had It," The Bell Notes (1959)
8. "M.T.A." The Kingston Trio (1959)
9. "Rescue Me," Fontella Bass (1965)
10. "Penny Lane," The Beatles (1967)
11. "Sixteen Tons," Tennessee Ernie Ford (1955)
12. "With a Little Help From My Friends," The Beatles (1967)
13. "U.S. Blues," Grateful Dead (1974)

CHAPTER 10:

Long-Term Care:
The Long and Winding Road

"There are only four kinds of people in this world—those who
have been caregivers, those who currently are caregivers, those
who will be caregivers and those who need caregivers."
—Former First Lady Rosalynn Carter

If you were born between 1946 and 1964 or thereabouts, you know that you are a part of the baby boomer generation, but do you know what it is to be part of the "sandwich" generation?[9] This term is defined not so much as people born in a certain time period as it is people who fall within a certain age bracket in their family line. A person in the sandwich generation has an aging parent to care for, as well as either a child under the age of eighteen to raise or an adult child to support in some way. The "sandwiched" life is common among the baby boomer generation as we deal with parents

---

9   Merriam-Webster officially added the term to it's dictionary in 2006.

who are living longer than previous generations and adult children who are taking a longer time to gain financial independence. While this increase in longevity is great news for our parents and for us, the fact that younger generations are having a more difficult time achieving financial independence is placing an unprecedented financial strain on our generation—a strain that many of us did not anticipate as we worked to first build our financial base and then invest in it for the future.

When You're the Bologna in the Family Sandwich

My bologna has a first name, it's O-S-C-A-R. My
bologna has a second name, it's M-E-Y-E-R.
—*"Oscar Meyer Bologna Commercial Song," Daniel Bedingfield (1974)*

For those baby boomers who are sandwiched between taking care of both their aging parents and their still-dependent older children, it can become increasingly difficult to make ends meet without depleting their retirement savings or their own health.

In fact, a recent report found that being a caregiver can have a tremendous physical and emotional impact and that the strain of it can shave years off of a caregiver's life.

While you never really plan on becoming a caregiver, there are things that can be done to mitigate the circumstances when they arise, and having some planning techniques might help relieve some of the stress and tension that naturally occurs.

In my own family, our household is about as multigenerational as it gets. We are blessed to have my wife's mother Carole (a.k.a "Nani"), our daughter Jessica along with her soon-to-be-husband Steven, and their son Julian. The house is plenty big for all of us to coexist, and it doesn't hurt that "Nani" makes the best spaghetti and meatballs you're ever going to eat! Several years ago, when we built the home, we had it designed with the goal of having Carole live with us for the remainder of her life—even if and when she requires some degree of caregiving. At present, she is at the spry age of eighty-five, but if that ever changes *we do have a plan.* Brenda's two sisters, brother, and their spouses, who all live locally, will pitch in and help Brenda, along with outside assistance if needed. We hope Carole can live out her life in dignity with her family. I know that even the best plan of this type has its foibles. People don't always get sick or die in the order that we think they should. Who knows if one of us may end up needing care instead of Nani? I also realize that many families don't enjoy the luxury of having members nearby who can lend a hand if necessary. Over the span of my professional career and even within my extended family, I have witnessed the physical and emotional drain that caregiving can have on everyone involved. Sometimes the caregiver ends up in worse shape than the person receiving the care. I'm certain that more than a few of you reading this can attest to that.

Here are four takeaways that I hope you will consider:

1. Planning for caregiving should start by talking about it *before it is needed.* Attempting to plan for something after it happens is called *damage control!* Be sure to include the person who may need the care in the discussion if that is possible.

2. Seek the council of a professional financial advisor to set up and moderate the discussion. This is of particular importance if you think it might become contentious among certain family members.

3. The financial cost of caregiving can be substantial, however, it can me minuscule when compared to the physical price that caregivers sometimes pay.

4. Have a Plan "B" in case Plan "A" fails. Remember that you can't have a Plan "B" unless you have a Plan "A".

Beyond the Bucket List

These happy days are yours and mine (oh, happy days).
— *"Happy Days Theme Song," Pratt & McClain (1976)*

When retirees and preretirees think about how they'd like to spend their retirement days, they typically think about positive things like traveling, spending more time with the grandkids, getting a vacation home, or buying new things. I doubt anyone has ever answered the question, "What do you want to do in retirement?" with, "Well, I'm definitely looking forward to years of immobility and incontinence and that happy time when my mental facilities decline and old-age frailty sets in."

No one ever talks about these things happening, but they are realities, and they need to be dealt with. As an advisor, I tell my clients that I'll work hard to help them complete their retirement bucket list, but they also have to agree to speak with me about what they expect to do when those other, not-so-enjoyable events start to happen.

This is the essence of the longevity risk—you'll live a long time and at some point during that time, something is going to happen. Don't risk everything that you've built up over your lifetime, because you didn't have a plan in place. Something is going to happen either way, so wouldn't it make sense to talk about it now, have some contingencies in place, and share your wishes with your family so that when something does happen, there's a plan in place to minimize the effect?

Planning for Long-Term Care

I've long since retired and my son's moved away. I called him
up just the other day. I said, 'I'd like to see you, if you don't
mind.' He said, 'I'd love to, Dad, if I could find the time.
—*"Cat's in the Cradle," Harry Chapin (1974)*

It's surprising how often I'll speak with the adult children of a parent who might need care and discover that those children have neither talked with each other about their caregiving plans nor with their parents.

About 90 percent of the time I'll sit down with the parents and say, "I talked to your kids, and they shared some ideas on how they want to help you in the future. By the way, did they ever ask you how you'd like to be cared for?"

In most cases, the answer is no.

Too often, the kids don't go to Mom and Dad; they just have their own ideas and make their own decisions, much as we did for our kids when they were little.

Unfortunately, this can become divisive for families. Mom might want to stay in her own home, but the kids are insistent that she live with them. If Mom is adamant, the kids might throw up their hands and walk away. The kids divorce themselves from their parents because they think Mom and Dad just aren't listening, when the fact is that sometimes the kids are the ones who not only aren't listening, they aren't even asking their parents what they want in the first place.

The first thing to do is acknowledge that your parents are getting older, and before something happens, you may benefit from all of you sitting down and talking about your plans with your advisor, who can serve as a mediator. If, after discussing as many of the possible circumstances that might arise, your parents still want to stay in their home as long as possible, then so be it. But before you walk away from the discussion, make sure you have the answers to two very important questions:

1. How is your parents' care going to be paid for?
2. Who is going to provide the care and how?

Most family members will say that they'll take care of Mom or Dad, but when the dominoes really start to fall, that doesn't always happen.

When helping your parents plan for long-term care, the best thing you can do as their child is to not assume that you know best. Don't try to make decisions for your parents when they're still able to make decisions for themselves, don't assume they've already got a plan, and be sure to work with an advisor to determine what's feasible and affordable when they do need to be under someone's care.

The Awkward Conversation(s)

It's vital for children and parents to sit down and discuss issues such as finances and the possibility of long-term care in a proactive way. This can be both awkward and is often very emotional. I know this because I have sat in on many as a facilitator and moderator. When I believe there could be future problems through what might be a lack of communication, I am not bashful about trying to get the family together to talk. Trying to figure out what to do before something happens can be a challenge, but attempting to sort things out after the fact can be overwhelming for everyone involved. Families need to have this conversation so parents can express *how they feel about their care* if something happens and how they plan on paying for it. I've seen families pulled apart because they couldn't agree on their parents' care, but I've also seen families smoothly make the transition because they took the time to have that awkward conversation.

As part of your own planning for the possibility or some not-so-good days down the road, it's not only important to make sure you have all of your legal documents in place but also to have that admittedly awkward conversation with your kids, clearly defining how you want to be cared for should something happen. Having all of these mechanisms in place helps to make the process as painless as possible for everyone involved.

"And Now the End Is Near?"

If you have aging parents, please don't assume that everything is set up the way it should be. End-of-life planning might be hard to bring up, but let me give you one bit of advice; *"Just because mom and dad haven't talked about it doesn't mean they haven't thought about it!* They have. They may be reluctant to bring it up because they're afraid that you might think one of them is in dire straits. If you want to get the conversation going, just ask them to read this chapter, then ask them what they think. And if by chance you're in or approaching that "aging parent" category yourself, have at least one of your kids read this chapter and tell them you want to talk about it. If all else fails, give me a call, and I'll get the ball rolling. We can guide you and your family in the right direction. I'm confident that you'll be glad you did.

To Pre-Pay or Not Pre-Pay...That Is the Question

I'm often asked if I recommend a pre-planned/pre-paid funeral. In most cases I usually respond with a resounding yes! As with any planning technique each case is different and there are exceptions but from a practical and financial perspective it often makes sense. The way I see it, the last big bash we're ever going to have is our funeral. Why allow someone else to plan it if you can do it yourself? Make it a sixties rock theme or mini-Woodstock if you like. Several of my friends in the funeral business say that more and more they're functioning as *event directors* and less as funeral directors. Today, many of us look at funerals as a way to celebrate the deceased person's life, which seems to be a much more pleasant way to let go of a loved one. Another advantage of prepaying is that it takes enormous pressure off the family in trying to decide what to do. A good friend of mine in the funeral business, Richard Reidy, has told me that when family members come in following the death of a loved one they don't always agree on how things should be handled. Lastly, and perhaps most importantly, please consider that the last memory your children have of you *should not be of picking out your casket!*

I encourage everyone who reads this to begin work on an *end-of-life plan.* An experienced advisor can help you get started and even sit in with you with your attorney and funeral professional if you like.

And please heed these words from an unknown poet:

> *The surest way to plan ahead*
> *Is get it done before you're dead!*

Not all of us have a clear warning forcing us to get our affairs in order. Instead of ignoring the inevitable, we should plan for it now, get it out of the way, and spend the rest of our time enjoying our bucket lists.

The Importance of Coordinating Financial Planning with Legal Documents

Several years ago, I received a call out of the blue from a man whom I had met with in the past along with his wife. He had previously told me that he wanted me to complete a financial plan for them but kept putting it off. Although I was surprised by his call, I had the perception that something had changed.

"Are you still interested in doing a financial plan for us?" he inquired.

"Of course," I told him.

"Well, when can you come over and get started?"

When I met with him and his wife, he looked perfectly healthy, but I had the feeling that something was up. There was urgency in his demeanor. When I completed the plan, which included a review of his legal documents, I returned to the house and reviewed it with him and his wife. When she stepped out of the room to answer the phone, he reached over to place his hand on mine and said, "Danny, my wife and kids don't know yet, but I've been diagnosed with pancreatic cancer. I'm dying of it. My doctor says six months at most. That's why I wanted to get things in order."

I swallowed hard and assured him that in my opinion things were in order. When his wife returned, he never let on. I don't know why, but he chose not to tell his adult children until the disease had taken hold several months later and he was in the Cleveland Clinic. That's when his daughter, who was also his durable power of attorney, called to let me know that he wanted me to come to the clinic and meet with them in his room. Understanding the gravity of the situation I rearranged my schedule and went the next day. When I got there, although he was sedated, he was cognitive and seemed at peace with himself. On the table was the financial plan binder I had previously completed. He told me that his wife was not emotionally able to be there and wanted me to go over things with his daughter. Then he thanked me for the work I had done. When I left the room, I knew that I would never see him alive again.

The fact is that, in many cases, adult children and sometimes spouses don't know about the household's assets—and liabilities if there are any. And I'm still surprised by how many people don't have their end-of-life legal documents in order (if they have them at all).

I've had numerous people call over the years and say, "Danny, Dad's passed away, and Mom's in ill health. We don't know anything about their finances—do you have that information to share with us?

As much as I'd like to help, in the absence of properly drafted legal documents, such as a durable power of attorney, advisors and financial institutions can't divulge that kind of information. The result can be long and costly, and estate issues could have been avoided with some basic planning. Thank goodness that in the story I shared with you the daughter was the power of attorney, so I could work with her.

Quick Riffs:

As much as we like to think about all the happy times we'll have during retirement, the fact is that we'll also have some unhappy times, such as when frailty sets in and long-term care is necessary. Instead of ignoring it, make a plan now so that everyone is on the same page when the inevitable occurs. When speaking with your advisor about your own or your parents' long-term care plans, consider the following questions:

- Do you know what your parents really want, or have you told your kids what you really want to happen when your health declines?
- Who is going to provide your long-term care?
- How will long-term care be paid for, regardless of whether you stay at home or move into a nursing-care facility?
- Have you assigned durable power of attorney so that your children have access to all of your assets?

Four Steps of End-of-Life Planning

1. Financial and legal planning
2. Medical care decisions

3. Housing decisions
4. Funeral planning

Caregiver Statistics

In 2009, about 42.1 million family caregivers in the United States provided care to an adult with limitations in daily activities at any given point in time, and about 61.6 million provided care at some time during the year. The estimated economic value of their unpaid contributions was approximately $450 billion in 2009, up from an estimated $375 billion in 2007.

Caregivers of older adults (age 50+) are likely to be taking care of their mother (34%), grandmother (11%), or father (10%). Many older care recipients are widowed (52%). More than half (53%) live alone.

Average age of today's caregiver is 50, and the average age of today's care recipient is 77.[1]

Duration of Care for Recipient:
*   34% - 1+ Years
*   31% - 1-4 Years
*   29% - 5+ Years
*   5% - Occasionally

Studies show that care giving compromises health.
About 60 percent of caregivers show clinical signs of depression.[2]

[1] *National Alliance for Caregiving (NAC) and AARP Caregiving in the U.S. 2009 (Bethesda, MD: NAC; Washington, DC: AARP, November 2009). Caregiving in the U.S. is an in-depth survey of 1,480 caregivers, weighted to be a nationally representative sample.*
[2] *Evercare® Study of Caregivers in Decline Findings from a National Survey September 2006 Evercare in collaboration with National Alliance for Caregiving*

Playlist:

1. "The Long and Winding Road," The Beatles (1970)
2. "Those Were the Days," Mary Hopkin (1968)
3. "When I'm Sixty-Four," The Beatles (1967)
4. "As Tears Go By," Marianne Faithful (1965)
5. "Cat's in the Cradle," Harry Chapin (1974)
6. "My Way," Frank Sinatra (1969)
7. "2000 Man," The Rolling Stones (1966)
8. "Happy Days Theme Song," Pratt & McClain (1976)

Watchlist

1. *The Sunshine Boys* (1975)
2. *What Ever Happened to Bay Jane?* (1962)
3. *Over the Hill Gang* (1969)
4. *Lost Horizon* (1937)
5. *The Picture of Dorian Gray* (1945)

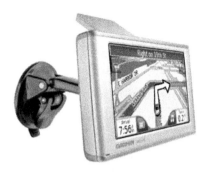

Don't Just Pack Your Bags; Plan Your Trip

If you don't take anything else away from this book, I would hope that you take away these two points:

- You are probably going to live a long time—a lot longer than you think. Plan for it.
- If you have reason to believe that you might not live a long time because of your health, there are still things that could be done to help you make the most of your life and finances while you are still able to do so.

The importance of planning and preparation are immeasurable, but you can run into problems if you're only planning *to* retire instead of planning what you're going to do *after* you retire.

Take, for example, the planning and preparations that my daughter and her family were making recently for a trip to visit relatives in Puerto Rico.

Because they live in our house, it was a real joy to see their excitement firsthand and to watch our grandson, Julian, pack for the trip. It's fascinating to see how a little one thinks he ought to pack for a trip; he must have emptied and repacked his pint-sized suitcase a hundred times in the days leading up to their departure.

It can be the same way with people planning to retire. They spend so much time anticipating their arrival at retirement that they don't plan what their life is going to be like once they do. Planning to retire is not the same as retirement planning.

Do you know what your financial world will look like on the day after you retire? What about in five years or ten years? Have you anticipated anything other than the target of retiring?

For most people, the answer is no. They're so busy packing and unpacking, like my little grandson, that they forget to think about what their retirement is going to look like once they arrive and how they're going to manage it for the long term, including what they're going to do when their health declines.

As I write this in early 2016, the stock market is down for the year and the Dow Jones is down about 10 percent. Another advisor just called me to ask how I would have answered a question that some clients of his recently put to him about their retirement plan.

The wife, he explained, is retired completely and the husband works part-time "just for the heck of it." They've started to draw down on their 401(k), which is 100 percent invested in mutual funds. When they looked at their statement recently, they saw that it was down 10 percent. They'd already taken out about 5 percent of the plan's value this year, which was in the $500,000 range at the beginning of the year. So essentially their retirement plan, which is supposed to last the rest of their lives, lost 15 percent—which equated to $75,000—of its value in just their first year of retirement. No wonder they were concerned!

When she called my advisor associate, the wife asked if they should stop taking money out of their plan until the market comes back and, in that regard, when would the market come back.

"What would you have told them?" he asked.

I thanked my advisor friend for thinking of me; I'm always honored when one of my peers reaches out to me for help. Then I reminded him that my response would have to be general in nature because I didn't have a complete picture of his client's situation, and I had never met them. Doctors don't provide specific diagnoses or treatments until they have first examined the patient. Advisors follow the same rule of thumb. General suggestions are fine, but specific advice should only be given when an advisor is in possession of all of the facts.

To her first question, I suggested to my friend that he invite both of them in for an evaluation of all of their assets, not just the 401(k) that had taken a tumble. He could start by reviewing their long-term goals and what might need to be modified on the short term to help them recover and then offer reassurance that, with some patience and planning, things could improve. I reminded him that, as advisors, sometimes the most important thing we can do for our clients is to hold their hands (figuratively speaking) and then make reasonable suggestions on how to move forward.

To her second question about when would the market come back, I postulated that when I'm asked that type of question my response always is, "I don't know!" I said that if his clients were in my office, I would explain that *there is no predictable, verifiable way to time the market*. If there is no way to accurately predict when it will go up (and there isn't), then it follows that there is no way to predict when it will go down. At that point I would ask them for the information I needed to evaluate their situation such as their ages, overall health, long-term objectives, risk-tolerance, other assets, income sources, current and potential future expenses, and anything else that might affect their future. Only then could I make recommendations that were based on the facts I had gathered and the feelings of the couple—not on when I thought the market was going up!

My advisor friend thanked me for my advice. I think he needed the same thing that his clients needed, which was a logical way to move forward and some reassurance. What I hope you take away from this is that a trusted advisor can help you navigate through the inevitable storms that all of us face as we go through life. And, like my advisor friend who called on me for advice, we take our responsibilities to our clients seriously, even to the point of reaching out to our associates for help when needed.

Most of us find it hard to let go of preconceived notions about what we believe to true. Thus the age-old question and response: Q: Why are you doing it that way? A: Well, that's the way we've always done it. As an advisor, one of the most poignant questions I ask perspective clients is, "Are you willing to consider advice from me even if at times you don't agree with it?" Most people respond with something like "Well, yes Danny, that's what we expect, I have to admit that every now and then I get a response like "I don't know, I'll have to think about that." It makes me wonder, why would anyone want an advisor if they don't want advice? Hmmm. Returning to the previously discussed couple, their $500,000, which is now down to about $425,000, could go down to $350,000 or $300,000 over the next couple of years if the market continues to do poorly. Even then, if the market starts to improve, they're no longer building on $500,000; they're building on a diminished $300,000. Within ten years, it's possible that their entire $500,000 would be depleted.

When I help people plan for retirement, or if I'm evaluating for people already retired, I always ask them to avoid cutting down the tree that feeds you. At retirement, one option would be to convert the growth in your investments to lifetime income by using properly funded income annuities. These can help you determine your base income, which you can match with other income sources such as guaranteed pensions, Social Security, or other sources.

Doing this—leaving your tree in place so that you can continue to harvest from it—means you don't have to sweat it when the market drops. Investments should be allowed to do what investments do and not be morphed into income. Don't create risk for yourself by doing this. Instead, take the risks off the table and leave that risk to be managed by people trained at risk management: the insurance industry.

Why Risk Your Retirement Income?

When it comes to financial planning, I'm a firm believer that while there may be a time to take risk, retirement is the time to take as much risk off the table as possible. What that couple could have considered would be to utilize certain types of annuity contracts that guarantee income payments for your lifetime (that can be adjusted for inflation) that are not negatively affected if the market tanks. One option would be to leave the remainder of their assets invested for potential growth and access later on in hopefully their long-term future. I don't know what you've read or heard about annuities, but for people who think that this might not be a wise choice, consider the fact that many major corporations such as Ford, General Motors, and Verizon[10] have transferred their pension liabilities to the insurance industry, which in addition to being best suited to managing risk is required to adhere to strict federal and state guidelines to protect the policy owners. This type of strategy is called Pension Risk Transfer because it utilizes group annuity contracts to transfer the pension risk from the corporation to the insurance company.

---

10   Timothy J. Geddes, Bradley B. Howard, Anthony G. Conforti, and Allison R. Steinmetz, "Pension Risk Transfer," Deloitte Consulting LLP, 2014.

What this means is that, if you're a pensioner for one of these companies, you shouldn't have to worry that your company's pension obligation could become underfunded and/or cut because the market is underperforming or because the company was improperly managed. Instead, they let the insurance industry handle their pensions through an annuity product—and the insurance industry has never, ever, failed to meet its obligations (at least not to my knowledge).

So consider harvesting only what you gain and decreasing risk to your retirement income. By so doing, you may be able to live comfortably knowing that you don't have to worry about the status of the stock market having a negative impact on your retirement savings.

The Grand Illusion

Don't be fooled by the radio, the TV, or the magazines.
—*"The Grand Illusion," Styx (1977)*

Many years ago, there was a TV commercial with a soap opera actor in a physician's white-coat stating, "I'm not a doctor, but I play one on TV." He then proceeded to hand out what sounded like medical advice about the product he was pitching.

Suppose that fellow, or one like him, advised a room full of people suffering from severe migraine headaches, telling them to take two of these headache pills, but no, you can't call him in the morning, because he's not really a doctor. What would you think? What would you do?

In reality, doctors have a saying: Know thy patient. In my business there is a requirement to "know thy client." This means that licensed financial advisors are obligated to not give *specific advice* to people without first learning about them and their individual objectives, risk tolerance, income needs, and other factors including health. Just as a good doctor wants you to have a physical and maybe x-rays and other diagnostic procedures before prescribing treatment, a financial advisor has to perform what I call a *financial physical* prior to making suitable recommendations.

When you hear people handing out random advice in some form of media or at seminars, you might inquire if they are licensed in the field that they claim to be an expert in. My friend Marty Higgins, a financial advisor in New Jersey, says, "It's amazing what you can say without a license." That's not to say that all of that type of advice is bad. In fact, you could learn some things. But as Shirley Ellis sang in her 1964 hit, if you "want to get down to the real nitty-gritty," at a minimum I suggest that you consider meeting with an advisor in your area to see if it makes sense to move forward. And please feel free to contact me personally.

Confident financial advisors are as open to you interviewing *them* as they are to interviewing *you*. If an advisor told you, "I can't give you specific advice because, well, I'm not really an advisor, but I play one on TV," you would probably laugh your way out of the office.

Some media-darling financial gurus will package and sell their information with an "opportunity" to purchase their done-for-you set of financial-planning videos, worksheets, and instruction manuals. And while I have no issue at all with the information contained therein, which is generally pretty broad, the fact is that for a similar price you could enlist the services of a dedicated financial advisor who gets to know you personally and then puts together a plan specific to your needs and objectives.

Through my membership with national financial associations, such as the Million Dollar Round Table and the Society of Financial Service Professionals, I have been able to meet advisors from all over the world. In talking with them, I've found that if there is one thing we all share in common, it's our commitment to being there when we're needed most—when life's events start to happen. Happy times or sad times, your advisor can be there to help you get through. All you have to do is pick up the phone.

It pays to plan, and it pays to have a professional helping you clearly define your needs and goals; because if you don't plan now, or you plan poorly, you will most certainly pay for it later.

Plan Now or Pay Later

If you had a hundred people in a room and you asked them all to write down one thing they would do in retirement that would help assure them of a happy retirement, you would get a hundred answers. Of those one hundred people, however, many of them would not have taken specific action to determine if those things could happen. Ultimately, the cost of having a plan in place is miniscule compared to the cost of not having one. It's why we pay for things like health insurance or home insurance. The cost of not having it in place could be tremendous, so we pay now to avoid the greater cost down the road.

The point is that proper retirement planning can give you:

- direction
- a feeling of confidence about how much you can spend and what you can do
- options to pursue your dreams

Because what a proper retirement plan does is help you avoid running out of money in retirement and maps out your wishes for the contingencies that inevitably come with age. You plan now to avoid the cost of ignorance and misinformation down the road.

Are You Ready to Rock and Roll Your Retirement?

Whether you are thinking about retirement or already retired, if you came in for a complimentary Discovery Session and asked for my advice as to the single most important thing you should do moving forward, my answer would be; "Let's sit down and figure out what you're trying to do! Let's talk about your dreams and aspirations, your family, your beliefs, your outlook on life, your health. Let's talk about how long you expect to be around—and anything else you want to share. Let's talk about the things that worry you, the risk that things could go wrong in your future and how to deal with those types of events. You can ask me questions, pick my brain, talk about whatever's on your mind—including reminiscing about the era of classic rock! I provide this at no cost or obligation whatsoever.

Then, if you decide to engage me as your advisor, I will explain to you exactly how I am paid. And yes, you can think about it if you want to—no worries. My only objective the first time we meet, whether in person, on the phone, or via Skype, is to have you feel better for spending the time with me.

In conclusion let me remind you that the part of your life called retirement is, to reference the Paul McCartney tune, a "Long and Winding Road." It might be wise to map it out—or better yet have a trusted advisor to be your "GPS" on your trek.

If you have questions about what you've read in this book or if you would just like to share a favorite rock and roll memory and talk about the glory days when rock was young, you can email me at danny.dfg@adviser-focus.com or call 1-800-783-2061.

Tell me what you think, tell me how you feel, tell me what's happening in your life, and if you enjoy the conversation and are in need of an advisor, I can work with you no matter what state you live in. The first session is complimentary. Remember, there's no time like the present to get rockin' and rollin' on your ideal retirement plan.

A Note About Social Security Planning:

There is a reason that I have not devoted a lot of space to Social Security planning. Simply put, the complexities of choosing the best Social Security strategy "for you" is beyond the scope of this book. There are in fact complete books on the subject that, after you read them, you might be even more confused! Suffice to say that there are multiple pathways and an informed/educated strategy may increase the total amount of benefits received over a lifetime (or joint lifetime). The best advice I can give is "don't decide until you're sure!" Often the best way to be sure is to have a knowledgeable financial advisor complete a personalized Social Security evaluation based on your personal situation. We have experience in this area and can help.

Note: I offer securities and advisory services through Mutual of Omaha Investor Services, Inc. Member FINRA/SIPC. Daniels Financial Group and Mutual of Omaha Investor Services, Inc. are not affiliated.

About the Playlists

Remember back to the glorious days of just three TV networks all in living black and white programming? There was a first-rate police drama series that ran from 1958 to 1963 called *Naked City* (based on the 1948 movie). The show always ended with the narration, *"There are eight million stories in the naked city…this has been one of them."* Well, if there are eight million stories in the naked city there are possibly an equal number of classic rock tunes that tie in (more or less) to the contents of this book. And because the classic rock era also includes classic folk, country, show, and movie tunes, the list is even longer. I'm certain that some readers may think, *Why didn't Danny refer to this tune or that tune in his book?* The answer is, there just isn't enough room! I found myself waking up in the middle of the night with a tune in my head and trying to remember it in the morning. My editors finally said, "Danny, try and get a good night's sleep—we've got enough to work with."

Also, some tunes I chose would probably not pass today's litmus test for political correctness. They were used *tongue in cheek* to (hopefully) make a point and lighten things up a bit.

I realize that some of the songs that appear have been recorded (covered) by multiple artists or recorded by the same artist more than once. For example in 1971 the tune "Do Ya" was released in the United Kingdom by a group called the Move on the B-side of "California Man." You've never heard of the Move? You're not alone. A few years later the group's lead singer, Jeff Lynn, formed one of the great rock groups of the 1970s, Electric Light Orchestra. ELO's version of "Do Ya" has become arguably the group's most recognizable tune. Then there's the Johnny Rivers 1964 smash-hit "Memphis." It's the story of a forlorn divorced father trying to reach his six-year-old daughter, begging the operator to, *"try and put me through to her in Memphis, Tennessee!"* The tune was written by Check Berry and appeared with little fanfare on the B-side of Berry's 1959 hit "Back in the U.S.A." It also was recorded as an instrumental in 1964 and was a hit for the recently deceased Lonny Mack. One person's B-side is another person's hit. Go figure!

Lastly, (and sadly) as hard is it may be to believe by today's standards, in the 1950s and to some extent into the early 60s many of the great tunes written and recorded by African American artists could not—or better stated—would not be played on many radio stations particularly but not limited to parts of the South. Because of this, white singers would record a "cover" of the tune so it could be played and ultimately sold to the "white markets." In my opinion one of the worst examples of this was Pat Boone's cover of Little Richard's "Tutti Fruiti." I have no gripe with Mr. Boone but come on; some things just weren't meant to be! Watch it on YouTube then watch Little's Richard's version and see what I mean. Rock and roll, with the help of many courageous DJ's such as Alan Freed, *American Bandstand's* Dick Clark, and the kids of that generation (us!) had a lot to do with helping to tear those walls down.

Resource List

Aging

https://www.ncoa.org/healthy-aging/

www.benefitscheckup.org

http://nihseniorhealth.gov/

http://www.seniordiscounts.com/

https://www.irs.gov/Individuals/Seniors-&-Retirees

Alzheimer 's Disease

www.alz.org

www.alzfdn.org

www.eldercare.gov

www.nia.nih.gov/alzheimers

www.nlm.nih.gov/medlineplus/alzheimersdisease.html

www.nia.nih.gov/alzheimers/publication/caring-person-alzheimers-disease

http://www.alzheimers.net/resources/

Caregiver

www.Medicare.gov/campaigns/caregiver/caregiver.html

http://www.aging-parents-and-elder-care.com/

http://caregiveraction.org/

Charity

http://www.give.org/
https://www.charities.org/charities

Divorced

http://www.divorcecentral.com/resource/organization.html
http://www.wiserwomen.org/index.
php?id=94&page=Divorce_&_Widowhood

Disability

https://www.disability.gov/
www.Ilru.org/html/publications/directory/index.html
www.mealsonwheelsamerica.org
www.seniortransportation.net

Long-Term Care

www.longtermcare.gov
www.medicare.gov/nursinghomecompare/search.html?
http://nihseniorhealth.gov/longtermcare
https://www.medicare.gov/coverage/long-term-care.html

Medicare/Medicaid

www.medicare.gov/Contacts/#resources/ships
www.smpresource.org
www.cms.gov

www.medicare.gov/homehealthcompare/

https://www.medicare.gov/forms-help-and-resources/index.html

https://www.medicare.gov/medicare-and-you/medicare-and-you.html

Prescriptions

https://www.medicare.gov/find-a-plan/questions/home.aspx

www.needymeds.org/inclusions/mission_statement.htm

Retirement

http://www.retirementjobs.com/

https://www.ssa.gov/retire/estimator.html

https://www.ssa.gov/retire/

https://www.irs.gov/Retirement-Plans/Plan-Participant,-Employee/
Saving-for-Retirement

https://www.irs.gov/Retirement-Plans/Plan-Participant,-Employee/
Changes-in-Your-Life-May-Affect-Retirement-Planning

http://askebsa.dol.gov/retirementcalculator/UI/general.aspx

https://www.usa.gov/retirement

https://www.alz.org/care/

Social Security

https://www.ssa.gov/

https://faq.ssa.gov/link/portal/34011/34019/ArticleFolder/421/
Social-Security-Number-and-Card

http://www.ssdrc.com/

Rock 'N' Roll is a tree with many branches
that grew from many seeds.

Its commemorative birthplace is Cleveland, Ohio.

Special Thanks to Our Friends at:

Oberlin, OH

Lorain, OH

www.RockinOnTheRiver.com

Rocky River, OH

www.becauseisaidiwould.com

Cover Photo Courtesy of:

www.facebook.com/EricaHCPhotography/